TRIPTYCH

Advent: 2022
Daily Advent Scripture, Reflection, and Prayer
(Includes Christmastide and Epiphany)

REVEREND STEVE HICKLE
ANDY MORRIS

Copyright © 2022 by WesleyMen, INC

All Rights Reserved. No part of this work may be reproduced or transmitted in any form or by any means, electronic or mechanical, including photocopying and recording, or by any information storage or retrieval system, except as may be expressly permitted by the 1976 Copyright Act or in writing from the publisher.

Request for permission can be addressed to:

WesleyMen, Inc. 3701 Hillsboro Pike, Nashville, TN 37215 or emailed to info@wesleymen.org.

ISBN: 9781734519921

Use of Scripture

Scripture used in this publication is from the Common English Bible (CEB) or the New Revised Standard Version (NRSV) unless otherwise noted.

New Revised Standard Version of the Bible. Division of Christian Education of the National Council of the Churches of Christ in the United States of America, Copyright 1989

The Common English Bible. The Common English Bible, Nashville, TN USA, Copyright 2011.

On The Cover

On The Move, 2022 by Ava Bryn Anderson, Digital Design

This triptych represents the three themes of this guide: Preparation, Celebration, and Migration. The panels depict new parents ready to welcome a child to be called Jesus, the generous gifts of the Magi, and the migrations/flight taken in scripture to places like Egypt, Judea, and Galilee (Nazareth).

Ava Bryn can be found on Instagram @cakestand.arts

ABOUT WESLEYMEN AND FASTPRAYGIVE.ORG

In 2021, between 701 and 828 million people faced hunger, according to the UN Food and Agriculture Organization (FAO). That's more than double the US population. 2 billion people globally are food insecure. Ours is the first generation on our planet that can end this horrific and intolerable situation. We grow enough food for ev-eryone. When we involve God and practice spiritual disciplines to align our lives and resources, we can deliver compassion and justice to help our needy neighbors.

The World Methodist Council passed a resolution in 2011 calling the people known as Methodists to **Fast** one meal per week, **Pray** during that time for world hunger, and **Give** to those in need. This became a global initiative of the World Fellowship of Methodist and Uniting Church Men (WesleyMen) and, as a re-sult, launched FastPrayGive.org.

This daily guide for Advent through Epiphany is a discipleship development aid. On the following two pages, you'll find ways that you can act during this season. We hope you will visit our website at FastPrayGive.org to learn more about our movement to end hunger by what John Wesley called "The means of grace." Or pick up our educational materials at **https://fpg.is/study**

Andy Morris
Director, FastPrayGive.org

andymorris@wesleymen.org

ACT: HELPING PEOPLE ON THE MOVE

On the web: **https://fpg.is/advent2022**

We offer specific appeals during Lent and Advent and encourage you to give during this season of reflection, anticipation, and meaning. In the past, we've worked with programs feeding people in Malawi, a hospital in Liberia, and the largest refugee camp in the world located in Bangladesh.

As of June 2022, The United Nations High Commissioner for Refugees (UNHCR) reports that 100 million people are displaced from their homes for the first time in human history. That is 1 in 78 people on earth. The total number of people displaced has reached a record high. The causes of people becoming persons of concern (refugee, asylum seeker, internally displaced, stateless) is varied. In the first half of 2022, we saw invasions, natural disasters, health emergencies, and political violence leading to people fleeing for safety, food, or opportunity.

UNHCR also reports only 53% of refugee sites surveyed had acceptable levels of food security. Access to clean water, healthcare, basic shelter, and the ability to work are all limited for displaced persons. https://fpg.is/unhcr-2021-report

We're asking you to consider a donation that will specifically aid displaced people. In addition, we'll match a total of all donations up to $3,000 from the World Wesleyan Hunger Fund. Our partner for this campaign is Church World Service (CWS). You may already know that CWS counts 37 denominations amongst its partners, including the African Methodist Episcopal, Christian Methodist Episcopal, African Methodist Episcopal Zion, and United Methodist churches.

A portion of the resulting grant to CWS will be directed to the Ukraine Crisis Response Fund to address the unique needs created by the conflict, with the rest of the funds unrestricted and applied as needed to CWS programs.

Learn more at https://fpg.is/advent2022

ACT: JOIN THE GLOBAL MOVEMENT TO END HUNGER BY THE MEANS OF GRACE

Fast one meal a week, Pray for the hungry and Give to people in need.

Go to our website, select a recurring monthly donation amount of as little as $8 a month, complete the registration form, and watch your inbox for information on weekly prayer and fasting.

It's that easy! We will reserve your monthly micro-donation to be disbursed via the World Wesleyan Hunger Fund to fight the systemic causes of hunger alongside inviting more people to join us in the means of grace.

CONTENTS

Introduction 8
First Sunday, November 27, 2022 10
Monday, November 28, 2022 12
Tuesday, November 29, 2022 14
Wednesday, November 30, 2022 16
Thursday, December 1, 2022 18
Friday, December 2, 2022 20
Saturday, December 3, 2022 22
Second Sunday, December 4, 2022 25
Monday, December 5, 2022 27
Tuesday, December 6, 2022 29
Wednesday, December 7, 2022 31
Thursday, December 8, 2022 33
Friday, December 9, 2022 35
Saturday, December 10, 2022 37
Third Sunday, December 11, 2022 39
Monday, December 12, 2022 41
Tuesday, December 13, 2022 43
Wednesday, December 14, 2022 45
Thursday, December 15, 2022 47
Friday, December 16, 2022 49
Saturday, December 17, 2022 51
Fourth Sunday, December 18, 2022 53
Monday, December 19, 2022 55
Tuesday, December 20, 2022 57

Wednesday, December 21, 2022	59
Thursday, December 22, 2022	61
Friday, December 23, 2022	63
Christmas Eve/Day, December 24/25, 2022	65
Monday, December 26, 2022	67
Tuesday, December 27, 2022	69
Wednesday, December 28, 2022	71
Thursday, December 29, 2022	74
Friday, December 30, 2022	76
Saturday, December 31, 2022	78
Sunday, January 1, 2023	80
Monday, January 2, 2023	82
Tuesday, January 3, 2023	84
Wednesday, January 4, 2023	86
Thursday, January 5, 2023	88
Epiphany, Friday, January 6, 2023	90
Want to Learn More?	93

Introduction

Welcome to *Triptych Advent:2022*! From the Greek *triptukhon*, "three-fold," a triptych is an art piece with three panels or sections, often hinged together literally and thematically. Such works of art emerged in the Middle Ages and have been around ever since. For us, a "triptych" helps name three interlocking or hinged seasonal themes. This *Triptych* is the fifth volume in this seasonal series. These daily readings span the first Sunday of Advent through Epiphany, November 27, 2022 – January 6, 2023, 40 readings in all. With this volume, we move to the third and final year of the *Revised Daily Common Lectionary* cycle (year A), delving deeply into Saint Matthew's account of events surrounding the Incarnation, Jesus' advent here.

While each gospel writer shared the same ancestral faith, Matthew's Jewishness seems more evident than that of Mark, Luke, or John. We will touch on themes he suggests by beginning the gospel with a "genealogy," one that connects Abraham to Jesus. In addition, Matthew stirs up holy memory from the prophets, citing their linkages to the Messiah.

As Matthew adds to the foundation for his gospel, he powerfully portrays God's gift of "dreams." With him and his Jewish readers, we might remember the ancestral Joseph and his brothers who pushed back on 'that dreamer.' Did 'our' Joseph also know that story? *Triptych Advent 2022* is built around that dream theme in three critical parts of the story:

- *Preparation* (**Joseph, marry Mary!**)
- *Celebration* (**Visit of the Magi**)
- *Migration* (**Egypt, Judea, Galilee/Nazareth**)

Ours is an attempt to read these holy scriptures in the framework, or worldview, of those who lived them. To help fill in the portrait/picture, we will need to draw from St. Luke, the other gospel author who portrayed this season in the life of Jesus and his family.

While St. Luke locates the story in the rule of Rome's Emperor Augustus and Syria's Governor Quirinius (NRSV), King Herod dominates St. Matthew's narrative. Herod's use (misuse) of power makes for a real and present threat to the young Jesus and his family. Threat and violence contrast starkly with our pageants' traditional tableaus but somehow resonate with people uprooted in our time. For displaced people, what becomes of their dreams, hopes, and desires to do good things for family and community?

Rooted in the Wesleyan tradition, we continually name the ways that movement has been at its best when becoming involved with these same marginalized. Is there not a shared longing for God's involvement with 'the least of these' – and with us? To deepen your involvement, please visit FastPrayGive.org.

From Advent's beginning through the Day of Epiphany, we will read a variety of powerful scriptures that give insight to people then and now who share the hope for "Emmanuel," that is, "God is with us." Together, let us also reflect, pray – and dream!

Reverend Steve Hickle, president

WesleyMen, World Methodist Council

Andy Morris, director

FastPrayGive.org

First Sunday, November 27, 2022

Read

The word that Isaiah son of Amoz saw concerning Judah and Jerusalem. In the days to come the mountain of the Lord's house shall be established as the highest of the mountains, and shall be raised above the hills; all nations shall stream to it. Many peoples shall come and say, "Come, let us go up to the mountain of the Lord, to the house of the God of Jacob; that he may teach us his ways and that we may walk in his paths." For out of Zion shall go forth instruction, and the word of the Lord from Jerusalem. He shall judge between the nations, and shall arbitrate for many peoples; they shall beat their swords into plowshares, and their spears into pruning hooks; nation shall not lift up sword against nation, neither shall they learn war any more. O house of Jacob, come, let us walk in the light of the Lord!
(Isaiah 2:1-5)

"But about that day and hour no one knows, neither the angels of heaven, nor the Son, but only the Father... Therefore you also must be ready, for the Son of Man is coming at an unexpected hour."
(Matthew 24:36, 44)

Reflect

Peace versus swords and spears may be the focus of many who read this scripture. Before we rightfully dive into our longing for peace, let us consider the city and a temple on a hill. The Babylonians, Sumerians, Canaanites, and countless other civilizations built their seats of power and prophecy centers (temples) upon hills. Jerusalem is on a hill, and the Temple of Jesus' day was upon its top. To visit these places, we must climb up, and whoever is 'up there' looks down upon all surroundings—a power move for sure. Jesus came to us from wherever God dwells. Suppose it's in a temple on a mountain, fine. Jesus came to us (down if you want a direction) to teach us to have compassion and fight FOR each other and not against one another. The prince of Peace is coming – if we accept him.

Pray

O Lord who comes among us as Christ incarnate, embodying the very love of God: now we enter this season of preparation. The prophetic word foreshadows your coming as the very Prince of Peace.[1] The prophet is not alone in envisioning swords reforged into plowshares, spears into pruning hooks,[2] weapons of violence visioned as implements for agriculture. Why, Lord, do we wait to 'implement' the vision? Why do we endlessly delay the holy way for us? We confess that even now, heavy armor rolls across borders, nations rise up against nations, and all military expenditures far surpass any humanitarian help. Has the very 'milk of human kindness'[3] soured? Evaporated? Dried up? Must the vision remain only a dream? When you come, Lord Jesus, what will you find? Take hold of these weary hearts, we pray, and frame them once more in the hope of peace. Stir in our dreams ways to actually turn 'weapons of mass destruction' into 'masses of human disarming'! It is our prayer that at your coming, you will find the faithful at the forge, where

> *They (we!) shall beat their (our!) swords into plowshares,*
> *and their (our!) spears into pruning hooks;*
> *nation shall not lift up sword against nation,*
> *neither shall they (we!) learn war any more.*
> Come, LORD Jesus! Amen.

---

1 Isaiah 9:6
2 Micha 4:3
3 Shakespeare, William. Macbeth.

Monday, November 28, 2022

Read

At the end of forty days Noah opened the window of the ark that he had made and sent out the raven; and it went to and fro until the waters were dried up from the earth. Then he sent out the dove from him, to see if the waters were still on the face of the ground; but the dove found no place to set its foot, and it returned to him on the ark, for the waters were still on the face of the whole earth. So he put out his hand and took it and brought it into the ark with him. He waited another seven days, and again he sent out the dove from the ark; and the dove came back to him in the evening, and there in its beak was a freshly plucked olive leaf; so Noah knew that the waters had subsided from the earth. Then he waited another seven days, and sent out the dove; and it did not return to him any more... Then God said to Noah, "Go out of the ark, you and your wife, and your sons and your sons' wives with you. Bring with you every living thing that is with you of all flesh – birds and animals and every creeping thing that creeps upon the earth so that they may abound on the earth, and be fruitful and multiply on the earth." (Genesis 8:6-12; 15-17)

Reflect

I had a dream of a flood the night before writing this. It was meager in comparison to the tale of Noah's encounter with destruction. In waking, I recalled the waters rose so fast but took so long to recede. The waiting to rebuild, the waiting for the drying and recovery. So much waiting. Noah, the families, and the animals waited to start a new life. Today we wait for the coming of Christ, both in the replaying of anticipation of the Messiah and the anticipation of the return of our Savior. Like Noah, we send out and are sent into the world to restore and recover a broken world in God's name.

Pray

Lord, we enter into an old story, one from the Book of Beginnings. Perhaps we've known it since childhood. On the one hand, its frame of destruction is hardly bedtime reading, but we've always loved the animals – and at least some, and someone, gets to begin again. Let us consider Noah, the raven, the dove – and ourselves. Surely, Noah never dreamed of what was to come – look where his obedience got him! God spoke, he listened, and was sent: sent to build a vessel, sent to gather his family and creatures in pairs, and as the rains fell, he was sent upon the waters. When adrift, can one dream of only water and waves, rain and more rain, overflowing the earth? When adrift on such unknown waters, of what future can one possibly dream? Like Noah, one might partner with a raven, one that goes 'to and fro,' much as we do when 'at sea,' seeking, searching – sinking. One might test another partnership, this time a dove that goes 'to and fro,' first frustrated, then bringing the sure sign of the water's ebbing. Noah was both sent and sender, one who sought and was sought by these creatures. Are we now asea, adrift with 'water' rising? As we wait for your coming, Lord Jesus, seek even us, send even us, and save even us. Amen.

Tuesday, November 29, 2022

Read

Then God said to Noah and to his sons with him, "As for me, I am establishing my covenant with you and your descendants after you, and with every living creature that is with you, the birds, the domestic animals, and every animal of the earth with you, as many as came out of the ark. I establish my covenant with you, that never again shall all flesh be cut off by the waters of a flood, and never again shall there be a flood to destroy the earth." God said, "This is the sign of the covenant that I make between me and you and every living creature that is with you, for all future generations: I have set my bow in the clouds, and it shall be a sign of the covenant between me and the earth. When I bring clouds over the earth and the bow is seen in the clouds, I will remember my covenant that is between me and you and every living creature of all flesh; and the waters shall never again become a flood to destroy all flesh. When the bow is in the clouds, I will see it and remember the everlasting covenant between God and every living creature of all flesh on the earth." God said to Noah, "This is the sign of the covenant that I have established between me and all flesh that is on the earth."
(Genesis 9:8-17)

Reflect

Most covenants make stipulations upon one or more parties. Most contracts include an offer, consideration, acceptance, and mutuality. Here, God offers assurance without any request for consideration on the absolute qualification of **all** *flesh on earth*. That is astounding. I'm not here to explain why a rainbow in the sky isn't a binding contract. I'm here to point out that it's a one-sided promise without a request to reciprocate. Yet, here we are, made in God's image. Should we not do likewise and promise to love, care for, and protect **all** our neighbors and world?

Pray

Gracious Lord, who is so very patient with us: we confess that we would move quickly to the 'rainbow '(and the 'manger'), failing to pause to ponder the arduous journey from here to there. Our toy arks and paired animals might remove us from the devastating deluge attended by death. It is painful to picture people up trees, on rooftops, fleeing for high ground, all surrounded by overwhelming waters. But that, too, is in the story. Here we remember the Lord God adamantly and repeatedly naming the *covenant* – seven times – that is, that agreement between 'unequal' parties, one in which God would prove to clearly be the more invested. After all, God is God, and we, well, we are still us. God has placed in the skies a kind of memo-to-self, every rainbow, to remember that covenant. God reassures Noah's people that never again will *God* cause the flood to overtake us – or the birds or domestic animals or every animal of the earth. But the seas are rising, are they not? For island nations, for coastal people, for lowlanders everywhere, is the die cast? Let us sit with that awhile – thinking about our shared human responsibility in that 'never again.' Then help us, Lord Jesus, to add to our season of preparation a new resolve to be good stewards, better stewards, great stewards of all that our God has made. Come among us, Lord Jesus. Amen.

Wednesday, November 30, 2022

Read

*This is like the days of Noah to me:
Just as I swore that the waters of Noah
would never again go over the earth,
so I have sworn that I will not be angry with you
and will not rebuke you.
For the mountains may depart
and the hills be removed,
but my steadfast love shall not depart from you,
and my covenant of peace shall not be removed,
says the Lord, who has compassion on you.*
(Isaiah 54:9-10)

Then the sign of the Son of Man will appear in heaven, and then all the tribes of the earth will mourn, and they will see 'the Son of Man coming on the clouds of heaven' with power and great glory. And he will send out his angels with a loud trumpet call, and they will gather his elect from the four winds, from one end of heaven to the other.

From the fig tree learn its lesson: as soon as its branch becomes tender and puts forth its leaves, you know that summer is near. So also, when you see all these things, you know that he is near, at the very gates. Truly I tell you, this generation will not pass away until all these things have taken place. Heaven and earth will pass away, but my words will not pass away.
(Matthew 24:30-34)

Reflect

Two scriptures. Two signs. The sign in the sky reminds us that all of the life on earth is no longer threatened by God's anger.

And a sign in the heavens about God's love. In both, God's glory will be known, and there will be mourning. Isaiah and Matthew aren't necessary for us to understand loss, love, and grace. These are built into our understanding of life, and we embrace and lament a repetitive cycle. We begin our Christian year again, remembering a covenant and preparing for the arrival (soon) and departure (too soon) of God's Son.

Pray

Christ our Lord, fully human and fully divine, hear our prayer: let us consider both the *covenant of peace* and your *coming on the clouds of heaven*. We are awed by the power of these moments paired here for our meditation. We confess that we too readily leap to the *covenant* (rainbows!) without first recalling that "the earth was corrupt in God's sight, and the earth was filled with violence."[4] Lord? Is not that still the case? Does not coercive brutality threaten to wash over those least able to stay afloat? In Noah's time, creation began again, a kind of a reset, but first the waters: a deep and deadly deluge. The prophet names God's commitment to *never again* flood the earth *and* to set aside holy anger –anger surely wholly deserved from then until now. Today, have we not taken the *covenant* for granted? Have we paid little heed to the signs that point to changing seasons, let alone changes in our environment, changes we have wrought? We must admit the covenant has not removed our penchant for more corruption, more violence. Can we leave all that behind? Will we? Ever?

Jesus, we prepare for your coming, fig tree-like, for you come to leave winter's dormancy behind, to show new life and bear much fruit. We who wait in faith dare to claim the *covenant of peace* and your *coming*. Come, Lord Jesus. Amen.

---

[4] Genesis 6:11

Thursday, December 1, 2022

Read

*Give the king your justice, O God,
and your righteousness to a king's son.
May he judge your people with righteousness,
and your poor with justice.
May the mountains yield prosperity for the people,
and the hills, in righteousness.
May he defend the cause of the poor of the people,
give deliverance to the needy,
and crush the oppressor.
May he live while the sun endures,
and as long as the moon, throughout all generations.
May he be like the rain that falls on the mown grass,
like showers that water the earth.
In his days may righteousness flourish
and peace abound, until the moon is no more.
Blessed be the LORD, the God of Israel,
who alone does wondrous things.
Blessed be his glorious name forever;
may his glory fill the whole earth.
Amen and Amen.*
(Psalm 72:1-7, 18-19)

Reflect

The more I read Psalms like this, the better I understand how to pray. We need to ask God to give other people, the people we rely on to lead us, the ability to make decisions that benefit all – not only those who are in power. That means a leader who seeks equity and not just equality [that is, a level playing field but with help for the 'players' who need help]. A just world results in equality, but the means to that end are filled with pitfalls. We have to pray for the strength of those we entrust to persevere through the struggles. How do you pray for your leaders? To have them struck by lightning or guided by a vision of a just reality?

Pray

Christ our Lord, whose reign we claim now and forever: tradition says that the psalm is about an ascendant Solomon[5] Scripture remembers

Solomon's dream in which God asked the new king what he would like to effect his rule, a query he answered not with 'might' or 'wealth' but ' wisdom.'[6] The psalm endured as the hopes for the young king were in some ways answered, carrying over to the hopes for many kings to come. In naming the LORD, *the God of Israel,* the psalmist is clear that the people the king governs are God's – *yours:*

> *May he judge your people with righteousness,*
> *and your poor with justice.*
> *We admit that it could be our lament now as so very few of*
> *those who now govern also*
> *defend the cause of the poor of the people,*
> *give deliverance to the needy,*
> *and crush the oppressor.*

In our recent experience, the poor are under attack; the needy are blamed for their plight; the rulers are more apt to accommodate the oppressor, to cooperate rather than to crush. Have we-the-governed forfeited our voice, staying silent in the face of such suffering – so long as it is not our own? In this season, may you renew in us the dream of the young king, the dream of wisdom and righteousness, the dream of defending the poor, the dream of deliverance from all that oppresses the people. In your holy name we pray, Amen.

---

5   Since ancient times, a superscript "Of Solomon" has accompanied the psalm.
6   1 Kings 3:5-9

Friday, December 2, 2022

Read

*Truly, O people in Zion, inhabitants of Jerusalem, you shall weep no more. He will surely be gracious to you at the sound of your cry; when he hears it, he will answer you. Though the L*ORD *may give you the bread of adversity and the water of affliction, yet your Teacher will not hide himself any more, but your eyes shall see your Teacher. And when you turn to the right or when you turn to the left, your ears shall hear a word behind you saying, "This is the way; walk in it." Then you will defile your silver-covered idols and your gold-plated images. You will scatter them like filthy rags; you will say to them, "Away with you!" He will give rain for the seed with which you sow the ground, and grain, the produce of the ground, which will be rich and plenteous. On that day your cattle will graze in broad pastures; and the oxen and donkeys that till the ground will eat silage, which has been winnowed with shovel and fork. On every lofty mountain and every high hill there will be brooks running with water – on a day of great slaughter, when the towers fall. Moreover the light of the moon will be like the light of the sun, and the light of the sun will be sevenfold, like the light of seven days, on the day when the L*ORD *binds up the injuries of the people, and heals the wounds inflicted by his blow.*
(Isaiah 30:19-26)

Reflect

I learned about silage this year. A city boy, I've never had to feed the cattle in winter. I guess I assumed beasts ate grass all year because it is plentiful. When the hay and grass aren't enough, there are other ways. Silage can be anything. Weeds and wild plants apparently work just fine in tough times. Plucked at their height and swashed into pens or containers, then covered with material like thick dirt layers or plastic. The moisture and the bacteria let the greens ferment and stay preserved. It seems like an inexpensive way, in tough times, to store up necessary nutrients. However, it must be cut, transported, and stored. Like the disposal of idols and vigilant work of staying on the path set before us, it is work and sacrifice that allows for survival. Maybe, just maybe, if we keep our eyes on God and love our neighbors, we can find prosperity.

Pray

Lord, we pray as those from the depths of The Exile. Is it our God who gives us now *the bread of adversity and the water of affliction*? Our tears tumble forth from suffering just as theirs; our cries nearly match their own; our weeping has drained us. Is it not notable that they looked for a Teacher, just as you came to be known? A rabbi, or as Mary called you, 'Rabbouni'?[7] We are awed that we can look to you not just for turning to the left or the right but to righteousness, right living that is *the* way in which to walk. We confess with the ancients that we, too, honor idols – sometimes unwittingly. While theirs were 'veneered' with precious metals, many of ours are more subtle, masked, some with a faith-facade. Grant us the courage and strength to scatter such signs of our deep longings, our yearnings for guaranteed outcomes. Will not the God who comes *give rain for the seed with which you sow the ground, and grain, the produce of the ground, which will be rich and plenteous*? Domesticated creatures fill the landscape, even they will have enough to eat. For many of us, the *day of great slaughter, when the towers fall,* stirs the memory of a painful event[8] in our lives – reminding us that we are more akin to these exiles than we thought. As their season of darkness wore on and on, so does ours: invasion and killing, the uprooting of peoples, a changing climate, a persistent pandemic. Come among us once more, our Teacher, saying, *"This is the way; walk in it."*

---

7   John 20:16
8   September 11, 2001, the destruction of the 'Twin Towers,' New York, NY, USA

Saturday, December 3, 2022

Read

Comfort, O comfort my people,
says your God.
Speak tenderly to Jerusalem,
and cry to her
that she has served her term,
that her penalty is paid,
that she has received from the Lord's hand
double for all her sins.
A voice cries out:"In the wilderness prepare the way of the Lord,
make straight in the desert a highway for our God.
Every valley shall be lifted up,
and every mountain and hill be made low;
the uneven ground shall become level,
and the rough places a plain.
Then the glory of the Lord shall be revealed,
and all people shall see it together,
for the mouth of the Lordhas spoken.
(Isaiah 40:1-6)

This is the testimony given by John when the Jews sent priests and Levites from Jerusalem to ask him, "Who are you?" He confessed and did not deny it, but confessed, "I am not the Messiah." And they asked him, "What then? Are you Elijah?" He said, "I am not." "Are you the prophet?" He answered, "No." Then they said to him, "Who are you? Let us have an answer for those who sent us. What do you say about yourself?" He said,

"I am the voice of one crying out in the wilderness,
Make straight the way of the Lord..."'
as the prophet Isaiah said."
(John 1:19-23)

Reflect

Has anyone ever asked you 'who are you?' and 'what are you doing here?' I hope it was not because you were trespassing or breaking some rules. Jesus told us we might be in danger when his words come out of our mouths. We know that a message of love and grace can turn away wrath. It can also feed the anger of those who want no change in a hurting world. Speaking in a prophetic voice is not, however, about us, is it? We don't need to do anything other than confess like John. "I'm just here to tell people to be ready for Jesus."

Pray

Lord Jesus, Lord of even the wild places, we long to hear such a word as this:

Comfort, O comfort my people, says your God.

An exiled people heard that word in a wilderness traversed, in a distant land, in a place not their home. Had they indeed 'served their term,' punished for idolatry, unholy alliances, a religion that rang hollow with no regard for poor people?[9] The prophet said so, but clearly, it was not 'time off for good behavior!' Surely the way through the wilderness was the way of the Lord. The word of the baptizing John echoes the ancient hope. As you would be, Lord, was he not confronted by those sent to learn who he was – or, 'Just exactly who did he *think* he was?!' The gospel is quite clear that John did not see himself as the One to come, a coming hoped-for across generations. He was the one in whom the word of the prophet came alive:

"I am the voice of one crying out in the wilderness,
Make straight the way of the Lord..."'
as the prophet Isaiah said."

Much lies between us and where we hope to be. Our own "wildernesses" are places a-hungered, racially charged, climate-challenged, violence-filled. Let us hear anew the John-word of hope. No matter the surrounding, subsuming wilderness, Lord, you are coming! Cross the waste places with us, we pray. Amen.

---
9   Isaiah 58:1-14

Second Sunday, December 4, 2022

Read

A shoot shall come out from the stump of Jesse, and a branch shall grow out of his roots. The spirit of the L{\sc ord} shall rest on him, the spirit of wisdom and understanding, the spirit of counsel and might, the spirit of knowledge and the fear of the L{\sc ord} His delight shall be in the fear of the L{\sc ord}. He shall not judge by what his eyes see, or decide by what his ears hear; but with righteousness he shall judge the poor, and decide with equity for the meek of the earth; he shall strike the earth with the rod of his mouth, and with the breath of his lips he shall kill the wicked. Righteousness shall be the belt around his waist, and faithfulness the belt around his loins. The wolf shall live with the lamb, the leopard shall lie down with the kid, the calf and the lion and the fatling together, and a little child shall lead them. The cow and the bear shall graze, their young shall lie down together; and the lion shall eat straw like the ox. The nursing child shall play over the hole of the asp, and the weaned child shall put its hand on the adder's den. They will not hurt or destroy on all my holy mountain; for the earth will be full of the knowledge of the L{\sc ord} as the waters cover the sea. On that day the root of Jesse shall stand as a signal to the peoples; the nations shall inquire of him, and his dwelling shall be glorious. (Isaiah 11:1-10)

Reflect

Someone who judges not by what his eyes see or by what his ears[10] hear has a special gift. In fact, that type of gift is a level of discernment that, for the most part, is not inherently human. As we read the Hebrew Bible, we often hear of Kings who are

---
10   Isaiah 11:3

just and who offer justice. The good ones do no harm, and their discernment of Justice is a divine gift. It's why we anticipate the coming of the King of Kings, Jesus Christ.

Pray

As we rehearse your coming, *Lord* Jesus, the prophet, frames a remarkable scene. Some will be familiar with works of art depicting even animal animosity becoming amicable.[11] Here there are repeated pairings of predator and prey; in the new order, the old enmity evaporates. For One is coming with the *spirit of the Lord* upon him. He will be One with *wisdom and understanding, the spirit of counsel and might, the spirit of knowledge and fear of the Lord.* The predator-prey relationship reversed, where the *wicked* powerful perish. It all comes to pass because our ancestors in the faith, the Israelites, prey to the predator, are about to rise. As cut off as a tree's stump, the 'dead' tree refuses to remain in death, sprouting forth – a sign of hope. As in the 'family tree' of the faithful,[12] the 'stump-shoot 'is reminiscent of Jesse's 'sprout' David, God's anointed – while still a child. The coming One is belted with, bound by, *righteousness* and *faithfulness.* He provokes the most extreme predators to turn away from violence: lion and lamb, leopard and kid, calf and lion… verily, the lion becomes a vegetarian! From what vantage point do we view such a Peaceable Kingdom? From here, we see that people-prey have little chance against the predator-people. While we may see ourselves as neither prey nor predator, both abound. Lord Jesus, flood us with this *knowledge of the Lord.* Cover us with it – worldwide, ocean-deep! May we protect the preyed upon, stand against the predator, until they prey no more. Come, Peaceable Kingdom; come, Lord Jesus. Amen.

---

11 e.g., search the works of Quaker minister Edward Hicks, "Peaceable Kingdom"
12 Matthew 1:5-6

Monday, December 5, 2022

Read

Finally, brothers and sisters, we ask and urge you in the Lord Jesus that, as you learned from us how you ought to live and to please God (as, in fact, you are doing), you should do so more and more. For you know what instructions we gave you through the Lord Jesus. For this is the will of God, your sanctification… that no one wrong or exploit a brother or sister in this matter, because the Lord is an avenger in all these things, just as we have already told you beforehand and solemnly warned you. For God did not call us to impurity but in holiness. Therefore whoever rejects this rejects not human authority but God, who also gives his Holy Spirit to you.

Now concerning love of the brothers and sisters, you do not need to have anyone write to you, for you yourselves have been taught by God to love one another; and indeed you do love all the brothers and sisters throughout Macedonia. But we urge you, beloved, to do so more and more, to aspire to live quietly, to mind your own affairs, and to work with your hands, as we directed you, so that you may behave properly toward outsiders and be dependent on no one
(1 Thessalonians 4:1-3a, 6-12)

"In everything do to others as you would have them do to you; for this is the law and the prophets."
(Matthew 7:12)

Reflect

I think Paul needs an asterisk by his last statement regarding 'living quietly.' It should say, "except in matters of justice where others have been exploited. In that case, we should make some noise. In that case, we should focus less on pleasing God." If our efforts to love one another mean we are seeking equity, then God will be pleased.

Pray

Lord of Thessalonica and every place on earth: we 'listen in' as St. Paul urges the faithful to *love all the brothers and sisters* and *to do so more and more.* There must have been no little tension in the young community, evidenced by Paul's weighty, *that no one wrong or exploit a brother or sister in this matter, because the Lord is an avenger in all these things...* Wait – the Lord as *avenger*? That is a heavy consequence for what must have been (and surely is) a consequential wrong. Paul reminds us that there is an accounting for mistreating or exploiting, other people. It is discomfiting to know that using people for one's own ends has such a long history. But how, Lord, do we answer the call to such a life of *holiness*, a life Paul starkly contrasts with one of *impurity*? As he reminds us that they (and we also) have the instructions for loving the brothers and sisters, one wonders if all that had been set aside. Paul's message leads to this: *so that you may behave properly toward outsiders...* Yes, Lord, you modeled for us proper behavior *toward outsiders*! At the very core of our faith is your own teaching, one that is shared by all the great faiths of the world:[13]

> "In everything do to others as you would have them do to you; for this is the law and the prophets."[14]

We pray that the outsiders be offered a welcome way in – today, tomorrow, always. Amen.

---

13 Ethical Framework, Interfaith Alliance of Wake County, NC, USA, p. 4
14 Matthew 7:12 (Sermon on the Mount)

Tuesday, December 6, 2022

Read

*Do not fear, you worm Jacob,
you insect Israel!
I will help you, says the Lord;
your Redeemer is the Holy One of Israel...
When the poor and needy seek water,
and there is none,
and their tongue is parched with thirst,
I the Lord will answer them,
I the God of Israel will not forsake them.
I will open rivers on the bare heights,
and fountains in the midst of the valleys;
I will make the wilderness a pool of water,
and the dry land springs of water.
I will put in the wilderness the cedar,
the acacia, the myrtle, and the olive;
I will set in the desert the cypress,
the plane and the pine together,
so that all may see and know,
all may consider and understand,
that the hand of the Lord has done this,
the Holy One of Israel has created it.*
(Isaiah 41:14, 17-20)

Reflect

The water, you say? Yes! We are so thirsty. Moreover, it's that valuable resource amongst others that seems to come from places where we just don't expect it. All these resources aplenty are a balm to weary generations of people returning from exile. Do we consider ourselves in exile today? Is our world ready to be reshaped to provide all that we need? God had the power, and through Jesus, we are given compassion and grace.

Pray

Lord Jesus, who knows well both *wilderness* and *desert*, you would know if the people 'saith unto' Isaiah, "Yeah, right!" Just lately,[15] the prophet had proclaimed a new era, one in which geologic gauntlet of the wild places would melt away before them – valleys lifted, mountains lowered, rough-going smoothed – a straight way home. As if that were not enough to get the people moving, Isaiah spoke words of reinforcement. Yes, Jacob's offspring, you are not much, lowly even, as mere worms and insects, fearful before the devouring, despotic Babylon. But I'm here! Says the LORD. Poor and needy you may be, but get ready! Your quest for water will be answered with more than a few drops: *rivers*! *fountains*![16] *pools of water*! *springs of water*! Over against the desert's barren spaces, get ready for *cedar*! *acacia*! *myrtle*! *olive*! *cypress*! *plane*![17] *pine*! What a contrast: from slavery's season of scarcity to a hospitable highway home, complete with abundant water to drink and ample shade for rest. Let us who are now in dry *deserts* far from home dream such a prophetic word – and may it come to pass! Even now, the way home is prepared. Will you walk with us, Lord Jesus? Amen.

---

15 Isaiah 40:1-11
16 Perhaps 'artesian' wells; compare 'living water,' John 4:14, 'a spring of water gushing up'
17 A 'plane' is a large sycamore-like tree.

Wednesday, December 7, 2022

Jesus responds to the charge that "by Beelzebul" he casts out demons. The name has roots in the Canaanite god Baal, by the first century it was a name for Satan.

Read

"Or how can one enter a strong man's house and plunder his property, without first tying up the strong man? Then indeed the house can be plundered. Whoever is not with me is against me, and whoever does not gather with me scatters. Therefore I tell you, people will be forgiven for every sin and blasphemy, but blasphemy against the Spirit will not be forgiven. Whoever speaks a word against the Son of man will be forgiven, but whoever speaks against the Holy Spirit will not be forgiven, either in this age or in the age to come.

"Either make the tree good, and its fruit good; or make the tree bad, and its fruit bad; for the tree is known by its fruit. You brood of vipers! How can you speak good things, when you are evil? For out of the abundance of the heart the mouth speaks. The good person brings good things out of a good treasure, and the evil person brings evil things out of an evil treasure. I tell you, on the day of judgment you will have to give an account for every careless word you utter; for by your words you will be justified, and by your words you will be condemned."
(Matthew 12:29-37)

Reflect

First, Jesus says, "I take what the devil claims is his because I tied him up and took it back." Then Jesus lets loose and says, "But that doesn't mean you get to be cavalier about forgiveness just because you run in my crew." What we say and do still matters. Judgment comes regardless of the provision of grace. Take that to the bank.

Pray

Gracious Lord, they were coming for you! Your response was restrained – at first. We can scarcely imagine being accused of being in league with the prince of demons[18], but you were so charged. Why were they so convinced of your evil grounding in doing good? For you, it was pretty straightforward: a 'house' divided could not stand, nor could a house be easily plundered while its owner protected the home. Were they edging closer to *blasphemy,* condemning not only you but in you the very essence of God? It sounds almost like you're saying, 'I can take it, but do not offend the Holy Spirit.' That said, you turn the challenge toward them: see the good fruit? The healings? The demons cast out? How can that *good* possibly come from a *bad* tree? Bad tree, sure, bad fruit. But that is not what they were witnessing! And Jesus, you remind us of the baptizing John who also called out his own detractors with *you brood of vipers!* They were as snakes, venomous, seeking to poison *the good treasure* you came to share. *The good person brings good things out of a good treasure, and the evil person brings evil things out of an evil treasure.* In Advent, we realize that it is no small thing to cast unfounded blame and damning falsehood, even as we are inundated with just that. Where we have been a party to such, forgive us, we pray. There is an accounting: *…by your words, you will be justified, and by your words, you will be condemned."* Come, Lord Jesus, we stand with you. Amen.

---

18   Matthew 12:24

Thursday, December 8, 2022

Read

*Happy are those whose help is the God of Jacob,
whose hope is the L*ORD *their God,
who made heaven and earth,
the sea and all that is in them;
who keeps faith forever;
who executes justice for the oppressed;
who gives food to the hungry.
The L*ORD *sets the prisoners free;
theL*ORD *opens the eyes of the blind.
The L*ORD *lifts up those who are bowed down;
the L*ORD *loves the righteous.
The L*ORD *watches over strangers;
he upholds the orphan and the widow,
but the way of the wicked he brings to ruin.
The L*ORD *will reign forever,
your God, O Zion, for all generations.
Praise the L*ORD
(Psalm 146:5-10)

Reflect

The God of Jacob is many things. The Creator who made heaven and earth, the Sustainer who provides for all in need, the great King who will reign forever. I'm not sure what's left for us to do other than to live, be the personification of love, and praise God.

Pray

Holy Lord, Just and Merciful, hear our prayer. It's as if the psalmist saw you coming! Perhaps we can regard this reading as a Song of Advent. Did you learn this psalm? Was it among the many such things you learned from mother Mary?[19] Was it one of her favorites – or yours? We trust that she taught you well, so why not? The psalm is well-rooted in the prophetic word, just as were you. Was your mother anchored there as well? Did she also know the poetry of Hannah?[20] This psalm catches sight of so much of the work of God. It not only sings of it but teaches it to the generations! Did you learn right here the meaning of the "happy are" sayings, as the Beatitudes[21]?

Happy are those whose help is the God of Jacob,
whose hope is the LORD their God...

In a way, our Lord, as you were taught, so you became the actual 'bearer' of these tidings, this good news: of a God who executes justice for the oppressed, offers food for those in need, sets free from oppression, heals blindness, lifts up the lowly, watches over us, upholds widow and orphan, points to the coming ruination of the wicked.[22] In this season, Lord, may we 'sing' this song, preparing again for your coming again! Amen.

---

19   Luke 1:46-55
20   1 Samuel 2:1-10
21   Matthew 5:3-12; Luke 6:20-21
22   Isaiah 1:17; 55:1; 61:1; 29:18, 35:5; 1 Samuel 8a and Luke 1:52; 27:3; Isaiah 1:17,23

Friday, December 9, 2022

Read

So Boaz took Ruth and she became his wife. When they came together, the Lord made her conceive, and she bore a son. Then the women said to Naomi, "Blessed be the Lord, who has not left you this day without next-of-kin; may his name be renowned in Israel! He shall be to you a restorer of life and a nourisher of your old age; for your daughter-in-law who loves you, who is more to you than seven sons, has borne him." Then Naomi took the child and laid him in her bosom, and became his nurse. The women of the neighborhood gave him a name, saying, "A son has been born to Naomi." They named him Obed; he became the father of Jesse, the father of David.
(Ruth 4:13-17)

Reflect

You've got some confusing genealogy going on here, all started by the selfless act of a daughter-in-law. The mother-in-law is adopting a child, and the neighborhood women's club is allowed to name the kid. He's named Obed, or "servant," and yet we don't know why. It's hard for us to figure out how a grandchild can be a servant or a redeemer. So strange to us, but we don't understand the challenges applied to someone without a next-of-kin. All the head-scratching is just noise. What we can really see is that Ruth loves Naomi. They are family. They are not from the same people or connected other than by a vacuum, and a baby makes it better. As we await the coming of Christ, we can understand when a baby can make it better.

Pray

Loving Jesus: this is the season where we are most apt to locate you in a family. Mary we know, and Joseph, and the gospel mentions brothers and sisters,[23] but who else? Saints Matthew and Luke have offered us family trees[24] from Abraham and from Adam. Today we remember your ancestors Ruth and Boaz – and where they came from. Then as now, one's antecedents mattered – perhaps too much. Ruth was from Moab, a kind of a chronic enemy of Israel. It's always been hard to set aside old wounds, hasn't it? We listen with interest as Ruth marries what to her was a foreigner, this Mahlon, child of Naomi and Elimelech. Along with the sister-in-law Orpah and Naomi, Ruth knew the death of a spouse. We know the great vulnerability of widows in that world. Wasn't she at risk of hostility, of shunning, a foreign widow in a foreign land? By grace, Ruth would connect with Boaz, a kinsman of her husband, one who could and would 'redeem' inheritance lost. By them, Obed would be born, then Jesse, then David, the ancestor whose 'house' would live on in you, our Lord and Savior. Were you not sometimes called 'son of David?' We are reminded that 'otherness' like this foreignness is of no account in the eyes of God. When will we live as if that is so? As if displaced people, uprooted, just like Ruth, also truly matter? Thou knowest. Amen.

---

23 Matthew 12:46-47
24 Matthew 1:1-17, Luke 3:23-38

Saturday, December 10, 2022

Read

John said to the crowds that came out to be baptized by him, "You brood of vipers! Who warned you to flee from the wrath to come? Bear fruits worthy of repentance. Do not begin to say to yourselves, 'We have Abraham as our ancestor'; for I tell you, God is able from these stones to raise up children to Abraham. Even now the ax is lying at the root of the trees; every tree therefore that does not bear good fruit is cut down and thrown into the fire."

And the crowds asked him, "What then should we do?" In reply he said them, "Whoever has two coats must share with anyone who has none; and whoever has food must do likewise." Even tax collectors came to be baptized, and they asked him, "Teacher, what should we do?" He said to them, "Collect no more than the amount prescribed for you." Soldiers also asked him, "And we, what should we do?" He said to them, "Do not extort money from anyone by threats of false accusation, and be satisfied with your wages."

As people were filled with expectation, and all were questioning in their hearts concerning John, whether he might be the Messiah, John answered all by saying, "I baptize you with water; but one who is more powerful than I is coming; I am not worthy to untie the thong of his sandals. He will baptize you with the Holy Spirit and fire."
(Luke 3:7-17)

Reflect

The last time we hear "brood of vipers" was (checks notes) Matthew 12, but that's not happened yet if we were to line up early

Luke in the timeline. We think of Jesus as superior to all, but there is no doubt he was a student of his cousin John. John called 'balls and strikes.' He knew the people came to hear better angels shout down their demons. He also knew his words were a stop-gap and that a more permanent solution was needed for his wayward vipers.

Pray

Lord, 'cousin' John is forever linked with you, isn't he? He would say you two were as 'fire and water,' but here, he brings the fire! He confronts the viperous leadership that had slunk in to investigate him and his message. He dares to challenge them for their *fruit*, knowing all the while that it is rotten fruit, fruit gone bad. No one likes to be called out for producing the bad tasting, the gnarled, the stunted. 'And don't try to claim that birthright stuff! God can raise up these rocks as easily as God gave you life.' These were not alone in hearing; members of that crowd began to speak up, asking John what they should do. He had particulars: if they were affluent enough to 'have two coats, give one away.' 'Food? Share that, too.' When the gospel says *even tax collectors* stepped forward, Luke suggests they are the most unexpected. 'Collect what's assigned, that's all.' We note that 'even' soldiers joined John in the river, asking the same thing. 'Don't be extorters, don't threaten anyone, don't sow disinformation; you get paid, that's enough.' They are bound together by an utter unlikelihood that they will turn from evil, but there they are: waist-deep, submitting to John, beginning life anew. So, Lord, we marvel at this powerful prophet, one who dares to dream the God-dream in the light of day. Help us, *even* us, to hear the word! Amen.

Third Sunday,
December 11, 2022

Tradition: this Sunday is known as Gaudete (Gow-day-tay) (Latin: rejoice ye), as the church, like Mary, erupts in joy

Read

And Mary said,
My soul magnifies the Lord,
and my spirit rejoices in God my Savior,
for he has looked with favor on the lowliness of his servant.
Surely from now on all generations will call me blessed;
for the Mighty One has done great things for me,
and holy is his name.
His mercy is for those who fear him
from generation to generation.
He has shown strength with his arm;
he has scattered the proud in the thoughts of their hearts.
He has brought down the powerful from their thrones,
and lifted up the lowly;
he has filled the hungry with good things,
and sent the rich away empty.
He has helped his servant Israel,
in remembrance of his mercy,
according to the promise he made to our ancestors,
to Abraham and to his descendants forever."
(Luke 1:46-55)

Reflect

Mary could see it. Even in all the unexpected and immense changes coming into her life, she could still have the 10,000-foot view of God's mercy. In her eyes, the grace which is extended to the lowly and hungry is plain to see. She can see the bad folks, the powerful and proud scattered by God's hand. If only we could always see God through grace-tinted glasses – and sing those same praises. Let this season be the start of permanently opening our hearts to God's mercy and grace.

Pray

Lord Jesus, who knows all things, was your mother-to-be dreaming? Or was she speaking aloud the God-dream of her very soul, as the prophets before her? We recall that it was her encounter with her kinswoman Elizabeth (and not-yet-born John) that released from her this astonishing 'song.' We might hear in her song echoes of her faith ancestor, Hannah.[25] We can but marvel at the deep impact she had upon your faith formation. We dare to ask: did this song become a lullaby? Oh, the things we would ask her – if we could! How could she possibly have known the salvation that would come through you? Or that in her humility, you would find your own humility? Or that her very name would become a blessing – as long as God's mercy resounds for those who 'fear' God? Or the setting right of so much that was wrong – and that accomplished through you? We are awed by it all: the *proud* scattered, the *powerful* brought down, the *lowly* uplifted, *hungry* people filled with good things, *the rich* sent away empty? She must have taught you, modeled for you the sense of the eternal God's justice now, God's righteousness now. What must we do with all this? Remember and enjoy? Repeat and internalize? Lord, in your tender mercy, may we sing with Mary and make the song were our own – it is her gift to the generations! Amen.

---

25 The Song of Hannah, 1 Samuel 2:1-10

Monday, December 12, 2022

Read

*Shall not Lebanon in a very little while
become a fruitful field,
and the fruitful field be regarded as a forest?
On that day the deaf shall hear
the words of a scroll
and out of their gloom and darkness
the eyes of the blind shall see.
The meek shall obtain fresh joy in the LORD,
and the neediest people shall exult in the Holy One of Israel.
For the tyrant shall be no more,
and the scoffer shall cease to be;
all those alert to do evil shall be cut off –
those who cause a person to lose a lawsuit,
who set a trap for the arbiter of the gate,
and without grounds deny justice to the one in the right.
Therefore thus says the LORD who redeemed Abraham,
concerning the house of Jacob:
No longer shall Jacob be ashamed,
no longer shall his face grow pale.
For when he sees his children,
the work of my hands, in his midst,
they will sanctify my name;
they will sanctify the Holy One of Jacob,
and will stand in awe of the God of Israel.
And those who err in spirit will come to understanding,
and those who grumble will accept instruction.*
(Isaiah 29:17-24)

Reflect

References to Lebanon and Jacob aside, about which we can't expect to fully grasp the context, the promise of better times and situations fills Isaiah chapter 29. You ask, "Why do we read this during Advent?" Because it is how Jesus's contemporaries understood the coming of the Messiah to be. Good times are coming, the bad people are going to be dealt with, and we're all going to come together. To get there, everything is going to be turned upside down…figuratively.

Pray

Lord, we are struck by the many difficulties of 'exile.' Perhaps we have had a taste of such ostracism, dislocated as we are by much that is happening. The prophet knows us so well, we who also *err in spirit* and who *grumble* at any instruction. Like those exiles, there are substantial ways in which we are neck-deep in tyrants, scoffers, and evildoers. It's as if *those alert to do evil* never miss a chance! Denying justice, they have no shame. We count ourselves among those beaten, humbled by our overflowing need. Our good plantings of prayer and love and doing good seem to yield so little fruit. But in the midst of all that, we look to you, Lord, to come among us. As these forebears hoped against hope for deliverance, the end to their exile-shame, a way home, so do we. Though we are crestfallen, we hope, for we have already seen the works of your hands in our midst! You have shown us how to stand up before the empire, to stand tall in the presence of tyrants. We must confess that we lack your courage and, certainly, your faith. Is there hope we'll gain what we lack? Is a season of fruitfulness drawing near? Will hearing and sight be restored, gloom and darkness pass away? In Advent, we join ourselves with you. Come again, we pray! Amen.

Tuesday, December 13, 2022

Read

*As a deer longs for flowing streams,
so my soul longs for you, O God.
My soul thirsts for God,
for the living God.
When shall I come and behold
the face of God?
My tears have been my food
day and night,
while people say to me continually,
"Where is your God?"
...Why are you cast down, O my soul, and why are you disquieted within me?
Hope in God; for I shall again praise him,
my help and my God...
I say to God, my rock, "Why have you forgotten me?
Why must I walk about mournfully
because the enemy oppresses me?"
As with a deadly wound in my body,
my adversaries taunt me,
while they say to me continually,
"Where is your God?"
Why are you cast down, O my soul,
and why are you disquieted within me?
Hope in God; for I shall again praise him,
my help and my God.*
(Psalm 42:1-3, 4-6a, 9-11)

Reflect

The Psalmist asks when he will get to see the face of God. Is he so ready to be in God's presence because of the constant and real questioning of God by others? Such a sad and forlorn song of worry and agitation! My friends, we know that God is with us. The Holy Spirit of God is in our presence always. We don't need to *see* God to have *hope* because we know that God became human to walk with us, and Jesus promised to return. All this begins in the retelling of the birth of Jesus.

Pray

Our Lord, both prophet and prophesied, walk with us in this prayerful moment. We are at home with the psalmist who continually hears, "Where is your God?" He is twice taunted, hammered by the voices that decry the very existence of his God! No wonder that he and we, like that deer, yearn for a freshet flooding some parched place… a 'place' that is us – and a world dried up, devoid of devotion to our God. In Advent, the siren call of craven consumerism 'taunts' even us who call upon your name, inviting us to replace faith with foolishness. In a time that replaces the great Gift with gifts so small, we are as the one who cries out,

Why are you cast down, O my soul,
and why are you disquieted within me?
But twice taunted, this one twice declares,
Hope in God; for I shall again praise him,
My help and my God.

Will we hope and praise? Are we able to awaken the dormant dream of your coming? Of peace on earth? Of goodwill to all? Lord! Help us to claim your coming! Where is *our* God? May we testify that *our* God can be seen, even known in you! All praise to God! Amen.

Wednesday, December 14, 2022

Read

*Surely he has borne our infirmities
and carried our diseases...*
(Isaiah 53:4)

When Jesus had come down from the mountain, great crowds followed him; and there was a leper who came to him and knelt before him, saying, "Lord, if you choose, you can make me clean." He stretched out his hand and touched him, saying, "I do choose. Be made clean." Immediately his leprosy was cleansed. Then Jesus said to him, "See that you say nothing to anyone; but go, show yourself to the priest, and offer the gift that Moses commanded, a testimony to them."
(Matthew 8:1-4)

When Jesus entered Peter's house, he saw his mother-in-law lying in bed with a fever; he touched her hand, and the fever left her, and she got up and began to serve him. That evening they brought to him many who were possessed with demons; and he cast out the spirits with a word, and cured all who were sick. This was to fulfill what had been spoken through the prophet Isaiah, "He took our infirmities and bore our diseases."
(Matthew 8:14-17)

Reflect

Jesus touched a leper. Well, yeah. He did it to heal him, one might say. Remember, to touch someone who was unclean made YOU unclean. It was the belief of the day that God chose to make people this way, with horrible skin conditions, because of something they had done or said. They often accepted fate, even though they asked God for it to go away. Do we accept the suffering of others that we could relieve, also believing we can't stop it? Do we sit idly by as we ask God for our society's blights to be removed whilst simultaneously shrugging it off as "the way things are?"

Pray

Our Lord and Healer, they found you, didn't they? Wherever you were, word spread, and they gathered around in hopes of your healing touch. So many of their ailments were of the sort we might call 'incurable' – but in you, their diseases were overcome. Theirs were diseases like leprosy, which certainly could have been different than today's leprosy.[26] Damaging spirits were cast out, and all manner of sicknesses were *cured*. We are in awe! So often, these were strangers, numbered among those whom you'd never even seen, let alone known. But your heart was stirred just the same. This one from Peter's household doubtless held special meaning for you and the company of disciples. Her fevered infirmity met its match! When healed, she rose up to immediately begin to serve you, for, after all, you were a guest in her house. We are surrounded by diseases that, by all accounts, are incurable, intractable. From the time of Isaiah until our own, people of faith have waited for and watched for One who *has borne our infirmities and carried our diseases.* Your friend (and our Saint) Matthew made the connection: you are that One! Help us, our Healer, to do all we can to bring healing to those consumed by any diseases and, just as you did, offer to heal freely to those we do not even know – that is what you showed us. Together, we dream of freedom from illness. Come again, O Lord, our Healer! Amen.

---

26 Hansen's Disease, an infection caused by Mycobacterium leprae.

Thursday, December 15, 2022

You find here an excerpt from Matthew's 'genealogy,' you'll see the names in bold are non-Israelites.

Read

*...and Judah the father of Perez by **Tamar**, and Perez the father of Hezron*
*...and Salmon the father of Boaz by **Rahab**, and Boaz the father of Obed by **Ruth**, and Obed the father of Jesse, and Jesse the father of King David. And David was the father of Solomon by the **wife**[27] of Uriah...*
(Matthew 1:3,5,6)

Now before faith came, we were imprisoned and guarded under the law until faith would be revealed. Therefore the law was our disciplinarian until Christ came, so that we might be justified by faith. But now that faith has come, we are no longer subject to a disciplinarian, for in Christ Jesus you are all children of God through faith. As many of you as were baptized into Christ have clothed yourselves with Christ. There is no longer Jew or Greek, there is no longer slave or free, there is no longer male and female: for all of you are one in Christ Jesus. And if you belong to Christ, then you are Abraham's offspring, heirs according to the promise.
(Galatians 3:23-29)

Reflect

Two sets of scripture collide. We have a family history of Jesus' family, and Paul's breaking down the walls of familial understanding and putting us all together into Christ's family. How

---

[27] Bathsheba, wife of Uriah the Hittite

can lineage be so important *and* also so unimportant that we discount it if we belong, as Paul says, "to Christ?" If you've read our small group study on ending hunger, you know that we emphasize that we're all part of the human family. We're unquestionably linked by design as self-described Homo sapiens. Why? It is about faith being a more powerful connection than blood. Love is a more powerful bond than family. Togetherness is a more realistic reason to love one another than the categories used to divide us. Sure, family is good for us to see where it is we came from, but those with whom we find peace and grace are our future.

Pray

Lord of *all people*, walk with us as we consider what the scriptures mean. Both saints Matthew and Paul point to a time when one's ancestors, one's roots, were paramount. While some might 'adjust' a genealogy such as Matthew's, he is careful to name all these forebears, never mind that some were not 'children of Israel.' Each of them has a place among those who came before you, our Lord. Is it not notable that these several women who were 'other' each played an important role in our salvation history? Tamar set right things amiss. Rahab hosted and protected spies. Ruth, loyal to her mother-in-law, brought her home; by Boaz, Ruth helped redeem the family's loss. Bathsheba, caught up in the drama not of her making, mothered a wise king, David's successor. We could cite your many challenges to the dynamic of insider/outsider, from the 'magi' who sought you to a Canaanite woman; you ranged into Syria, the Decapolis, Gerasene, and all domains of Gentiles; you sowed a gospel seed in every sort of 'soil.' Paul's own "line" came from those who would exclude such from worship and pretty much from their presence. For him, the law that had governed from his ancestry until then held no power in the face of faith, that is, faith in you, the Messiah. In you, we are one: not Jew or Greek, not slave or free, not male or female – one. It is *you* who make us heirs of the promise, the long hoped for salvation. Come once more and free *us* from the constraints that bind *us*! Amen.

Friday, December 16, 2022

Read

*Give ear, O Shepherd of Israel,
you who lead Joseph like a flock!
You who are enthroned upon the cherubim, shine forth
before Ephraim and Benjamin and Manasseh.
Stir up your might,
and come to save us!
Restore us, O God;
let your face shine, that we may be saved.
O LORD God of hosts,
how long will you be angry with your people's prayers?
You have fed them with the bread of tears,
and given them tears to drink in full measure
You make us the scorn of our neighbors;
our enemies laugh among themselves.
Restore us, O God of hosts;
let your face shine, that we may be saved.*
(Psalm 80:1-7)

What do you think? If a shepherd has a hundred sheep, and one of them has gone astray, does he not leave the ninety-nine on the mountains and go in search of the one that went astray?
(Matthew 18:12)

Reflect

Sometimes I feel like I've been fed the same "bread of tears," the psalmist describes when I think of all those who suffer. There are days that I sigh so hard at the things that are not going well in our world, a sigh so hard that I shiver afterward. Is it just me? But the psalmist calls for God to shine on us. Doesn't it give us imagery of God in heaven, bright as can be radiating upon us like the sun? It doesn't matter how bad things have gotten. The face of Yahweh can save us. Why? Because our God will do anything for us. Even further, not just for us as humanity or a subset of people, but save us as individuals, restoring us as sheep to the flock.

Pray

Lord Jesus, whom we know as the *Good* Shepherd, consider us now your own 'flock.' The psalmist is in a low place, with prayers somewhere between unheard and unmet, prayers he feels are only answered angrily. We know that place! Was there war? Strife? Utter and endless disappointment? Yes, yes, yes. We understand that kind of confusion, as we, too, had thought of our shepherding God as a Benevolent One. With this one of old, we plead for a hearing. With many, we are tempted to use 'flowery' language in hopes of catching God's attention. We may even attempt to make a case for our own achievements, hoping God will notice. But before we claim the high ground, let's admit the low: in war, in hunger, in poverty, in uprootedness, we are accomplices – whether we admit it or not. We are part of systems that advantage some but disadvantage many. To honestly reckon with that, we must join the psalmist in tears; in our sorrow, our every drink, our very bread tastes of tears. Enemies laugh, neighbors scorn – but we are not alone. That is the dawning of the darkness. You, our Good Shepherd, have not abandoned us! As the generations before us, so now we pray,

Restore us, O God of hosts;
let your face shine, that we may be saved.

Come, Lord Jesus, the One in whom we know God. Shine upon us; save us, even us. Amen.

Saturday, December 17, 2022

Today's Isaiah reading, "Immanuel," is paired here with Sunday's gospel (Matthew) text, "Emmanuel," that is, "God is with us."

Read

Again, the LORD spoke to Ahaz, saying,
Ask a sign of the LORD your God; let it be deep as Sheol or high as heaven.
But Ahaz said, I will not ask, I will not put the LORD to the test.
Then Isaiah said: "Hear then, O house of David! Is it too little for you to weary mortals, that you weary my God also?
Therefore the Lord himself will give you a sign. Look, the young woman[28] is with child and shall bear a son, and shall name him Immanuel.
He shall eat curds and honey by the time he knows how to refuse the evil and choose the good.
For before the child knows how to refuse the evil and choose the good, the land before whose two kings you are in dread will be deserted..."
(Isaiah 7:10-16)

"Look, the virgin shall conceive and bear a son, and they shall name him Emmanuel[29]."
(Matthew 1:23)

Reflect

Isaiah makes some bold predictions regarding a sign that will be in the form of a child. It's not only a suggestion that someone will come and represent 'God with us' as the name suggests, but that the child will see disaster fall upon Israel in just a few

28 Greek, the virgin
29 God is with us

years. This prophecy, 800 years before Jesus, reverberates like an echo through time. Have we not compromised on *our* faith and begged for a sign from God many times over? Do we not still cry out to God for help but from a position of safety and comfort? We know that God is with us, and through this, all things are possible, and yet, we still need a sign.

Pray

Lord, your coming comes closer! As we ready ourselves to hear Joseph's dream, we rehearse the 'sign' given to Ahaz, king of Judah. As with rulers then and now, he was much concerned for the nations surrounding them. We know that the prophet addressed the matter, urging the king not to trust in foreign alliances but to trust in God. Speaking the word of God, Isaiah challenged Ahaz to ask for a sign of the Lord one high as heaven or deep as Sheol. Ahaz refused the offer, feigning faith with, *I will not ask, I will not put the Lord to the test.* The prophet persisted, promising a sign anyway! That sign would be the child, one bearing the name Immanuel, that is, "God is with us." But Ahaz would indeed put God to the test, would he not? We will learn that the king would ally himself with the powerful and aggressive Assyria, before whom the nations fell one by one, including his own. We can learn that Ahaz sought to appease the powerful by adding an altar in the temple and sacrificing to their captor's gods. Lord, do we not live in a time of unhappy alliances? Of unfaithful accommodations, sacrificing faithfulness for security? How hard to hear such a prophetic word! And how comforting it is when we do. For now, the season unfolds to the point of listening in on the same prophetic sign for Joseph:

"Look, the virgin shall conceive and bear a son, and they shall name him Emmanuel."

Come, Lord Jesus – Emmanuel! Amen.

Fourth Sunday, December 18, 2022

The first mention of the name Jesus, the Greek form of the Hebrew Joshua, "The LORD saves/helps."

Read

Now the birth of Jesus the Messiah took place in this way. When his mother Mary had been engaged to Joseph, but before they lived together, she was found to be with child from the Holy Spirit. Her husband Joseph, being a righteous man and unwilling to expose her to public disgrace, planned to dismiss her quietly. But just when he had resolved to do this, an angel of the Lord appeared to him in a dream and said, "Joseph, son of David, do not be afraid to take Mary as your wife, for the child conceived in her is from the Holy Spirit. She will bear a son, and you are to name him Jesus, for he will save his people from their sins." All this took place to fulfill what had been spoken by the Lord through the prophet:

*"Look, the virgin shall conceive and bear a son
And they shall name him Emmanuel,"*

Which means, "God is with us." When Joseph awoke from sleep, he did as the angel of the Lord commanded him; he took her for his wife, but had no marital relations with her until she had borne a son; and he named him Jesus.
(Matthew 1:18-25)

Reflect

Spoiler alert: Jesus is about to be born. I like how Matthew doesn't bury the lede. Why is it this way? Maybe it's because the circumstances around Christ's arrival are worthy of note. We need to know about Mary and Joseph, the conception via the Holy Spirit, and the prophecy it fulfills. Besides, it's not uncommon to tell people what they need to know multiple times. Dale Carnegie said it best, "Tell the audience what you're going to say, say it; then tell them what you've said." Don't take away from this the intricacies and the process of communication. Rather take away that the amazing story of God becoming human to rectify our broken relationship is so important that the 'delivery' has been significantly tuned for maximum effect.

Pray

Lord, just as in Joseph's awakening, you are ever closer to coming! Would that we could ask him about that holy dream. If he lay down to a troubled sleep, we would certainly understand. With Mary's news, their engagement was on shaky ground. We have not a clue as to how Mary's family received her 'announcement,'[30] or Joseph's either, for that matter. We might wonder if their families had arranged the marriage, as many did. How does one, even one with great faith, process information that is entirely counter to the norm? And custom? And religious practice? Did it occur to Joseph that God was doing a new thing? We must admit that in the face of all this, we, too, would be befuddled. Exhausted, Joseph slept. Wasn't the dream delivered by a dream angel, a holy messenger of God? The message was very direct: it's alright, *do not be afraid to take Mary as your wife* (Gulp! Really?), *for the child conceived in her is from the Holy Spirit* (That would be a *very* different thing!). *She will bear a son, and you are to name him Jesus, for he will save his people from their sins.* Gospel-writing Matthew jumps in here, 'like the prophet said:'

"*Look, the virgin shall conceive and bear a son,
And they shall name him Emmanuel,*"

reminding us *Emmanuel* means "God is with us." Thanks be to our living God. That was enough! Joseph awoke equipped with the word of the Lord to do *as the angel of the Lord commanded him*... What would we do with such a dream? Help us, Lord Jesus. Amen.

---

30 See the 'Annunciation,' Luke 1:26-38

Monday, December 19, 2022

Read

God also said to Abraham, "As for Sarai your wife, you are no longer to call her Sarai; her name will be Sarah. I will bless her and will surely give you a son by her. I will bless her so that she will be the mother of nations; kings of peoples will come from her." Abraham fell facedown; he laughed and said to himself, "Will a son be born to a man a hundred years old? Will Sarah bear a child at the age of ninety?" And Abraham said to God, "If only Ishmael might live under your blessing!"

Then God said, "Yes, but your wife Sarah will bear you a son, and you will call him Isaac. I will establish my covenant with him as an everlasting covenant for his descendants after him. As for Ishmael, I have heard you: I will surely bless him; I will make him fruitful and will greatly increase his number. He will be the father of twelve rulers, and I will make him into a great nation. But my covenant I will establish with Isaac, whom Sarah will bear to you by this time next year." When he had finished speaking with Abraham, God went up from him.
(Genesis 17:15-22)

Reflect

Ever notice how God breaks the news of unexpected babies on a one-on-one basis? God tells Abraham the same thing he had already communicated with Sara. The Angel tells Mary, and then Joseph gets the info in a dream. Would it not be more efficient to get them together and just tell them both at the same time? I imagine the looks exchanged between the couples as they are being told would be priceless. At the very least, we can imagine the exciting conversations once both parties know. How did that conversation between Sarah and Abraham go? Other than, "but we're old!" I'm sure they leaned on their faith and trust in God.

Pray

Soon, Lord, we'll mark your coming. As days of waiting wane, we turn to the ancestors, our faith is rooted in them. Are we startled to witness God meeting with Abraham – for a talk? It all seems so normal. The "news" God brings to Abraham, which he shared with Sarah, calls to mind the "news" Gabriel brought to your mother, Mary – who surely shared it with Joseph. For both: startling. Unsettling. Unexpected. Impossible. No way… right? But as both stories unfolded there was indeed a way, God's way, the way forward – for the whole of humanity. The people of promise would look back to Abraham and Sarah, even as they would look ahead to the Messiah. Abraham face-plants, then he laughs[31]. Both seem about right. He thinks of Sarah, who would be ninety when, or if, it all came to pass. And he'd be one hundred! But he already knew this God, didn't he? We might say, 'he went with it.' Therein lies the struggle for us. In the face of the startling, unsettling, unexpected, and even impossible, we're a bit more reluctant to 'go with it.' Remind us, Lord, of the sacred stories! Let us live what we have heard from the angel to your mother: *For nothing will be impossible with God.*[32]

---

31 Hebrew: yitskhaq "he laughed," giving the promised son his name. (The New Interpreter's Dictionary of the Bible, Vol. 3, p 70, Abingdon, 2008)
32 Luke 1:37

Tuesday, December 20, 2022

Read

The Lord dealt with Sarah as he had said, and the Lord did for Sarah as he had promised. Sarah conceived and bore Abraham a son in his old age, at the time of which God had spoken to him. Abraham gave the name Isaac to his son whom Sarah bore him. And Abraham circumcised his son Isaac when he was eight days old, as God had commanded him. Abraham was a hundred years old when his son Isaac was born to him. Now Sarah said, "God has brought laughter for me; everyone who hears will laugh with me." And she said, "Who would ever have said to Abraham that Sarah would nurse children? Yet I have born him a son in his old age."
(Genesis 21:1-7)

When his mother Mary had been engaged to Joseph, but before they lived together, she was found to be with child from the Holy Spirit. Her husband Joseph, being a righteous man and unwilling to expose her to public disgrace, planned to dismiss her quietly. But just when he had resolved to do this, an angel of the Lord appeared to him in a dream and said, "Joseph, son of David, do not be afraid to take Mary as your wife, for the child conceived in her is from the Holy Spirit. She will bear a son, and you are to name him Jesus, for he will save his people from their sins.
(Matthew 1:19-21)

Reflect

Oh boy, do names have meanings. Selecting a name for your child is a very important moment – and has repercussions. But our use of those names is developed further by those who carry them. No doubt, when God told Abraham about having a son at one hundred years old, he probably laughed. "Say what, God? Is this a joke? Did Hagar put you up to this? Funny stuff!" All kidding aside, that name associated with the child is 'one who laughs.' With names still holding meaning in our world today, do we not have lots of Isaacs and Jesuses with us today? Conversely, Adolph is all but unused, as Judas and Jezebel. Volumes could be written about names and their meanings, but our takeaway today is that Jesus comes to save.

Pray

Jesus, as your coming nears, we enter into an imagined moment. We wonder, what would it be like for your own mother Mary to sit together with Sarah, the mother of nations?[33] Surely by now, they've had time to do so! There is so much they share: possibility in impossibility, openness in improbability, faith, even in utter unlikelihood. In our memories, the one is forever young, the other the elder. Do they run into each other somewhere, and one says, 'Can we talk?' Why not? As well as we know their stories, we would gain a whole new hearing in listening to them tell it – just exactly how was it? This would be a mother-to-mother kind of chat. Mary would ask, how did you and Abraham meet? And Sarah asks, you and Joseph? How exactly did 'he' receive *your* news? At some point, Mary might say, 'you know, we should really bring cousin Elizabeth into this – you remind me of her so much! There might have been a time of talking baby names. 'O, there was no doubt! This 'child of laughter' would be Isaac!'[34] And, Oh, that Gabriel! He said, "you will name him Jesus."[35] So we did! And you know, the same thing Gabriel said to me would come to Joseph in a dream. Think of that!' Maybe they talk about how the 'saving from' goes to unthought-of places: from illness, oppression, injustice, hunger, and exclusion. We can wonder further if they meet often and sort through their wondrous stories – and those of others. We are called to do that, as the stories matter as much now as then. Come, Lord Jesus. Amen.

---

33 Genesis 17:16
34 Isaac's name means, "he laughs" (see Genesis 17:17, 18:12-15
35 Jesus, Greek form of Joshua, "God is salvation;" compare Luke 1:31, Matthew 1:21

Wednesday, December 21, 2022

Read

*"My heart exults in the LORD;
my strength is exalted in the LORD.
My mouth derides my enemies,
because I rejoice in my victory...
Talk no more so proudly,
let not arrogance come from your mouth;
for the LORD is a God of knowledge,
and by him actions are weighed.
The bows of the mighty are broken,
but the feeble gird on strength.
Those who are full have hired themselves out for bread,
but those who were hungry are fat with spoil...
The LORD sends poverty and wealth;
he humbles and he exalts.
He raises the poor from the dust
and lifts the needy from the ash heap;
he seats them with the princes
and has them inherit a seat of honor...
he LORD! His adversaries shall be shattered;
the Most High will thunder in heaven.
The LORD will judge the ends of the earth;
he will give strength to his king,
and exalt the power of his anointed."*
(I Samuel 2:1, 3-5a, 7-8a, 10)

Reflect

If this is your first Advent with us, you may recognize that we are convinced that Mary was super familiar with Hannah's song, of which you've just read a portion. The canticle found in Luke 1:46-

55 is Mary's tribute to the celebratory spirit which accompanied a historically miraculous birth. In both cases, these soon-to-be mothers see their children as a magnification of the Lord's goodness. (In fact, that is why Mary's song is called *The Magnificat*, from the first word of the 4th century Latin translation of the Bible.) I don't know if you've ever wondered if Mary could read, or had read Samuel, or if it was read often enough that she knew it by heart. Or is it the author Luke's fondness for Samuel or even Jerome's 'vulgate' translation that tied together these distinct but interlinked verses? Either way, we join Mary and Hannah's voices in singing God's praise.

Pray

O Lord, the time shortens when we will mark your coming. Consideration of your birth keeps drawing us to other memorable ones. Childbirth, while natural, is for many a challenge *in extremis*, or perhaps remains a dream. In your birth, we see *not* the 'usual' but rather the highly 'unusual,' a birth by which God is accomplishing the most remarkable. In God's work, there emerge certain patterns; we might suggest that your mother's response to her 'news' echoes that of Samuel's mother, Hannah, whose season is also akin to Mary's kinswoman Elizabeth.[36] We note that while clearly 'chosen,' neither mother trumpets herself – instead, both exalt and glorify and magnify God. We might also note that we have named their responses to God's mighty act a 'song,' one where each 'sings' praises, not just for God's touch upon them but also upon flawed humanity. For now, the Creator recreates, setting right that gone wrong: derisive enemies are themselves derided; the too-proud-too-loud are quieted, their arrogance dismissed; judgment by might yields to judgment by knowledge – by the All-Knowing One; coercive weapons break into pieces; those who have had their food served to them learn to work for it; people thrown-away as refuse are recovered, reseated; the dishonored honored. Those who have meted mighty 'justice' might melt awy – for *the Most High will thunder in heaven. The LORD will judge the ends of the earth...* In all honesty, we also tremble! But oh, how we long for your coming, Lord Jesus! Amen.

---

[36] Elizabeth, mother of John (the Baptist), Luke 1:5-25, 39-45

Thursday, December 22, 2022

Read

*Your eyes will see the king in his beauty;
they will behold a land that stretches far away.
Your mind will muse on the terror;
"Where is the one who counted?
Where is the one who weighed the tribute?
Where is the one who counted the towers?"
No longer will you see the insolent people,
the people of an obscure speech that you cannot comprehend,
stammering in a language that you cannot understand.
Look on Zion, a land that stretches far away!
Your eyes will see Jerusalem,
a quiet habitation, an immovable tent,
whose stakes will never be pulled up,
and none of whose ropes will be broken.
But there the Lord in majesty will be for us
a place of broad rivers and streams,
where no galley with oars can go,
nor stately ship can pass.
For the Lord is our judge, the Lord is our ruler,
the Lord is our king; he will save us.*
(Isaiah 33:17-22)

Reflect

Historically speaking, I'm not sure we, in our present-day situation, have a lot of connection to this section of Isaiah. Without understanding the context fully or going into a ton of detail, can you imagine that the author then was looking back and contrasting recent atrocities to his current day's reasonably 'okay' situation? For us, a list of communities disrupted by gun violence:

we can often look back and see the worst, but are we also looking forward to a vision of a better tomorrow with God? We are to be looking, seeing, and visioning a future where the ruler is God, who is just, and whom we rightfully know gives us hope in abundance.

Pray

Our Lord, today we are in the company of an expectant people, one whose wait stretches beyond our season's mere days to many decades. The prophet's people are exiled, far, far from home. They long for *land that stretches far away*, the memory of which is continually clouded by *terror*. They remember *Zion, Jerusalem, a quiet habitation;* their peaceful place, obliterated by warriors' onslaught, lies in ruins. They think of it as *an immovable tent,* recalling that movable wilderness 'tabernacle' of their ancestors, forebears whose 'exodus' delivered them from bondage. Now paying tribute to hold off the aggressors enslaves them once more. Their captors, these *insolent people*, could not be understood, let alone be dissuaded from overrunning their homes, their hearts, their holy place. It is to these devastated ones the prophet speaks. 'Let your eyes see what your memory sees,' he says. There is One who is coming – judge, ruler, king – the very-*Lord in majesty.* We can identify with these "besieged." While an army may not be at our door, such onslaughts are never far off, terrorizing in their destruction and death. No less than these ancestors, we, too, await salvation. We, too, are without power; but we, too, are not without hope! Come quickly, Lord Jesus! Amen.

Friday,
December 23, 2022

Today we borrow a reading from Christmas Eve to further amplify
The Nativity

Read

*The people who walked in darkness
have seen a great light;
those who lived in a land of deep darkness –
on them light has shined.
You have multiplied the nation,
you have increased its joy;
they rejoice before you
as with joy at the harvest,
as people exult when dividing plunder.
For the yoke of their burden,
and the bar across their shoulders,
the rod of their oppressor,
you have broken as on the day of Midian.
For all the boots of the tramping warriors
and all the garments rolled in blood
shall be burned as fuel for the fire.
For a child has been given to us,
a son given to us;
authority rests upon his shoulders;
and he is named
Wonderful Counselor, Mighty God,
Everlasting Father, Prince of Peace.
His authority shall grow continually,
and there shall be endless peace
for the throne of David and his kingdom.
He will establish and uphold it
with justice and with righteousness*

from this time onward and forevermore.
The zeal of the LORD of hosts will do this.
(Isaiah 9:2-7)

Reflect

Will and *shall* are used a lot in this section from Isaiah. Have you ever wondered why these words, which at the surface serve the same purpose, are so readily interchangeable and yet different? Legally speaking, 'shall' means there is an obligation or duty to perform or carry out an act. 'Will' simply means that the parties are willing to or have a strong desire, but there is no requirement. I think about this every time I read *"...and there shall be endless peace"* – and I'm waiting for that day. Come, Jesus, Prince of Peace. We're ready.

Pray

Our Lord, as the time nears, perhaps once again we have heard the sonorous strains of *Messiah*[37] – and have been wondrously uplifted. Many have suggested that composer and compiler were 'inspired,' that is, 'in-spirited' with the very breath of God. Arising from the prophet Isaiah, the prophecy has soared beyond the constraints of that moment (and its king rising) to embrace your coming – our Lord! As before, the prophet dreamed the God-dream out loud, and it has come to pass. For in you, we do know *now* the dashing of oppression – the shattering of 'yoke' and 'bar' and 'rod' – signs of enslavement, the strong dominating the weak. For you were, and are, the child among all children, the awaited one personifying the prophetic:

For unto us a child is born,
unto us a son is given;
and the government shall be
upon his shoulder:
and his name shall be called Wonderful,
Counsellor, The mighty God,
The everlasting Father, The Prince of Peace.[38]

In you, that word is made flesh and dwells among us! Come soon, Lord Jesus! Amen.

---

37 George Frideric Handel, composer, 1741, text compiled by Charles Jennens
38 King James Version, integral to G. F. Handel's Messiah

Christmas Eve/Day
December 24/25, 2022

Read

In those days a decree went out from Emperor Augustus that all the world should be registered. This was the first registration and was taken while Quirinius was governor of Syria. All went to their own towns to be registered. Joseph also went from the town of Nazareth in Galilee to Judea, to the city of David called Bethlehem, because he was descended from the house and family of David. He went to be registered with Mary, to whom he was engaged and who was expecting a child. And she gave birth to her firstborn son and wrapped him in bands of cloth, and laid him in a manger, because there was no place for them in the inn.

In that region there were shepherds living in the fields, keeping watch over their flock by night. Then an angel of the Lord stood before them, and the glory of the Lord shone around them, and they were terrified. But the angel said to them, "Do not be afraid; for see – I am bringing you good news of great joy for all the people: to you is born this day in the city of David a Savior, who is the Messiah, the Lord. This will be a sign for you: you will find a child wrapped in bands of cloth and lying in a manger." And suddenly there was with the angel a multitude of the heavenly host, praising God and saying, "Glory to God in the highest heaven, and on earth peace among those whom he favors!"
(Luke 2:1-14)

Reflect

I want to call out the storytelling 'device' I find annoying. A whole bunch of angels appearing and singing scared the fool out of the shepherds in the field – people that live outside against the threat of dangerous weather and wild predators. People today watch an excess of scary movies and ghost hunting shows on television. Do you think that our contemporary neighbors would be so afraid of such a sight today? In our world, for a lot of people, fear is welcomed and enjoyed. If we're not 'sore afraid'[39] of the unnatural sights and sound of heavenly hosts bringing good news, what might the telling of this story look like in today's time? What mechanism of 'fear' might be a delivery system for good news? A host of birthday party clowns? That scares me! Or is the fear a simple bit of arcane but authentic context? Set aside how the news comes to us and focus on the news itself. Christ is born.

Pray

Our Lord, the awaited time is upon us! The story begins with such difficulty. We are readily reminded of those who travel in the most basic ways: on foot or with the modest help of animals. Mary and Joseph could not have wanted to embark on such a journey, not then, not that way, not so very far. But that was the power of empire, demanding the unreasonable in unreasonable ways. St. Luke places side by side the most powerful, emperor and governor, and the most powerless, your family – and shepherds, laborers on the night shift. St. Luke says they were *living in the fields*; homeless? They kept moving to do a hard, thankless job. The Almighty God had a choice: share the news of your coming with the 'greats' or the 'in-no-way-greats.' There is a kind of symmetry between your family, demeaned Galileans, and these discounted sheep-keepers. And it is for them that the angel of the Lord and the very hosts of heaven erupt in the news, good news, great news! That heavenly 'flock' breaks forth in praise: *Glory to God in the highest heaven, and on earth peace among those whom he favors!* Atremble, 'sore afraid,' the shepherds will venture to Bethlehem anyway. As we settle into the joys of Christmas, grant us 'shepherd hearts:' with the holy announcement heard afresh, no matter our fears, we journey to you! For you are born, our Savior, our Lord. Amen.

---

39   Luke 2:9, King James Version

Monday, December 26, 2022

"The Feast of Saint Stephen, the first 'martyr,' is marked the first day after Christmas. A full reading of 'deacon' Stephen is found in Acts 6-7.

Read

Stephen, full of grace and power, did great wonders and signs among the people. Then some of those who belonged to the synagogue of the Freedmen (as it was called), Cyrenians, Alexandrians, and others of those from Cilicia and Asia, stood up and argued with Stephen. But they could not withstand the wisdom and the Spirit by which he spoke.
(Acts 6:8-10)

When they heard these things, they became enraged and ground their teeth at Stephen. But filled with the Holy Spirit, he gazed into heaven and saw the glory of God and Jesus standing at the right hand of God. "Look" he said, "I see the heavens opened and the Son of Man standing at the right hand of God!" But they covered their ears, and with a loud shout all rushed together against him. Then they dragged him out of the city and began to stone him; and the witnesses laid their coats at the feet of a young man named Saul. While they were stoning Stephen, he prayed, "Lord Jesus, receive my spirit."
(Acts 7:54-59)

Reflect

The Hellenistic Jewish people who had immigrated back from Greece and surrounding areas wanted to not appear to be a problem. The Hebraic Jews and Hellenistic Jews didn't always have the greatest relationship, and there was suspicion of those who'd returned as being too liberal. Clearly, Stephen struck a nerve. Replacing the norms in the synagogue with the idea that the Messiah was Jesus became a bridge too far. It doesn't feel like it's a stretch of the imagination that we could drown out the message of love and grace shared by Jesus (and Stephen) with cheers for "our side." How can we share the light if we're using it only to navel-gaze, that is, to look only at ourselves?

Pray

Lord Jesus, you are born anew! But oh, how bad are we at celebrating your birth? On this 'day after,' we are left with tree lights above and emptiness below. In truth, that emptiness may be something within us as well. Have we been more attached to the outer décor than the inner substance of this moment? This 'day after' is the moment the church recalls the faithful who began to step up – only to be struck down. It is the sainted Stephen whose story speaks first. Stephen is accused of replacing the Moses-faith in God with a Jesus-faith. False witnesses[40] are found to accuse him of tearing down all that has been built up, including the beloved temple and customs of the forebears. In Stephen, has not the church recognized a 'type' of you, Lord? For he is one *full of grace and power, (who) did great wonders and signs among the people*; near his end, he says, *"Lord Jesus, receive my spirit;"* at his death, just as your baptism, *the heavens opened*. For the generations, he is a witness that with the coming of the Light of the world, the powers of darkness have not given up. Those that stood against you continue to stand atop the faithful, those who would let your light shine. This deacon first called to serve the 'widows' could no more remain silent than Jeremiah.[41] These millennia later, we lament that death-by-mob is still with us. Help us to hear the full-throated witness of all the saints from then until now! For you are born, born anew. In you, all is *made* new. Amen.

---

40   Acts 6:13
41   Jeremiah 20:9, where the prophet's silence is as "a burning fire shut up in my bones"

Tuesday, December 27, 2022

Read

Praise the L{\sc ord}
Praise the L{\sc ord} from the heavens;
praise him in the heights!
Praise him, all his angels;
praise him, all his host!
Praise him, sun and moon;
praise him, all you shining stars!
Praise him, you highest heavens,
and you waters above the heavens!
Let them praise the name of the L{\sc ord}
for he commanded and they created.
He established them forever and ever;
he fixed their bounds, which cannot be passed...
Kings of the earth and all peoples,
princes and all rulers of the earth!
Young men and women alike,
old and young together!
Let them praise the name of the L{\sc ord},
for his name alone is exalted;
his glory is above earth and heaven.
He has raised up a horn for his people,
praise for all his faithful,
for the people of Israel who are close to him.
Praise the L{\sc ord}
(Psalm 148:1-6, 11-14)

Reflect

Much like pictures of cats or dogs doing cute things on social media, this Psalm contains the content we're here for. Often, we're left pondering the voice of the psalmist or the inflection which might be applied to understand the context. Here, there is no question. God has given us glory, and we all must praise Him!

Pray

Our Lord and Savior, let us, with the psalmist, reecho the strains of angels! How like the angelic heavenly host to now sing,

> *Praise the LORD from the heavens;*
> *praise him in the heights!*
> *Praise him, all his angels;*
> *praise him, all his host!*
> *Praise him, sun and moon;*
> *praise him, all you shining stars!*

All are called to sing the praises of this God who in you has now come among us to dwell and to remain. But how many will do that – really? We look to your faithful friend, Assisi's Francis, for help:

> *All creatures of our God and King,*
> *lift up your voice and with us sing,*
> *O praise ye! Alleluia!*
> *O brother son with golden beam,*
> *O sister moon with silver gleam!*
> *O praise ye! O Praise ye!*
> *Alleluia! Alleluia, Alleluia!*[42]

From both psalm and saint, we gain glimpses of creation's marvels. Even beyond these ancients' sense of *'fixed... bounds, which cannot be passed,'* we know now there is much more – from ocean deeps to deep space! And you, Lord Jesus Christ, are in all, through all, over all. We pray that we, with you, claim that now and always, for you are Lord! Amen.

---

42 United Methodist Hymnal, Abingdon, Nashville, TN, 1989, p 62

Wednesday, December 28, 2022

We will revisit this text, expanded, on January 1, the First Sunday after Christmas

Read

...And having been warned in a dream not to return to Herod, they left for their own country by another road.

Now after they had left, an angel of the Lord appeared to Joseph in a dream and said, "Get up, take the child and his mother, and flee to Egypt, and remain there until I tell you; for Herod is about to search for the child, to destroy him. Then Joseph got up, took the child and his mother by night, and went to Egypt, and remained there until the death of Herod. This was to fulfill what had been spoken by the Lord through the prophet, "Out of Egypt I have called my son."

When Herod saw that he had been tricked by the wise men, he was infuriated, and he sent and killed all the children in and around Bethlehem who were two years old or under, according to the time that he had learned from the wise men. Then was fulfilled what had been spoken through the prophet Jeremiah:

"A voice was heard in Ramah, wailing and loud lamentation, Rachel weeping for her children; she refused to be consoled, because they are no more."
(Matthew 2:12-18)

Pictured: Small Statue of Flight to Egypt

Reflect

We look back and see protection, not merely from an earthly father protecting his child, but God-provisioned protection. It is explicit. Go, go now, and here's why. Don't just go but go and stay there until you're told it's safe to come back. We see the fulfillment of prophecy, as Matthew explains, but what we possibly move past is the innumerable deaths doled out because of one man's outsized fear and ambition. May we lend our voices and support to those who mourn because their loved ones are no more – for no good reason.

Pray

On this day, Lord, we are offered 'The Feast of the Holy Innocents.' We have gathered many times among the grieving, often sharing food with them. But a 'feast' day? The passing of many centuries has not diminished the deathly pall shrouding this day. Lacking the support of home, with few kinfolks in Bethlehem, your family was in peril. Here we remember that, for a second time, Joseph listened to a holy dream – and acted in faith. By his God-guided hand, you were saved, carried to safety in that far land. Your journey is sometimes artfully depicted as *The Flight to Egypt*. Joseph protected you and Mary, for who could be more vulnerable to violence than an infant and a new mother? The faith community recalls those who died at Herod's hand, eighteen infants, tradition says. St Matthew reclaims our faith-mother Rachel's lament, born of the anguish as the children of Israel assembled to be exiled:

> *"A voice was heard in Ramah,*
> *wailing and loud lamentation,*
> *Rachel weeping for her children;*
> *she refused to be consoled, because*
> *they are no more."*

In their sacred memory, we lift up all children faced with violence. We pray that by your tender mercy, each will be delivered to safety. We pray in your name, O Holy Child of Bethlehem, Amen.

Thursday, December 29, 2022

Read

*Thus says the L<small>ORD</small>:
A voice is heard in Ramah,
lamentation and bitter weeping.
Rachel is weeping for her children;
she refuses to be comforted for her children,
because they are no more.
Thus says the L<small>ORD</small>
Keep your voice from weeping,
and your eyes from tears;
for there is a reward for your work,
says the L<small>ORD</small>:
they shall come back from the land of the enemy;
there is hope for your future,
says the L<small>ORD</small>
your children shall come back to their country.*
(Jeremiah 31:15-17)

As he came near and saw the city, he wept over it, saying, "If you, even you, had only recognized on this day the things that make for peace! But now they are hidden from your eyes. Indeed, the days will come upon you, when your enemies will set up ramparts around you and surround you, and hem you in on every side. They will crush you to the ground, you and your children with you, and they will not leave within you one stone upon another; because you did not recognize the time of your visitation from God.
(Luke 19:41-44)

Reflect

2022 became a year when we heard phrases in the daily news that had been silent for so long, "cut off from resupply" and "surrounded by forces." More recently, we've heard the echo of the "near destruction" of cities. In both cases, we've seen people who, as Luke put it, will "crush you to the ground." Why? Because we know Jesus lamented the lack of peace that has defined and will define the future of Jerusalem. How ironic, as Jerusalem as a word and a name shares a connotation of peace. Do we humans, makers of war, kill for salvation or judgment? When has it *ever* been righteous to do so?

Pray

Lord, Jesus, we witness weeping that is your own. We place you beside the 'weeping prophet' Jeremiah. Just as St Matthew, Jeremiah lays claim to the tears of our faith-mother Rachel, a mourning rooted in his time. We remember that you were not long past the 'entry into Jerusalem.'[43] Your own procession must be contrasted with the many grand entrances of the ruling Herod,[44] where pomp and might themed them all. Had the war-horse-mounted king known of your humble mount, would he have been tweaked? Probably. Would it have worried him that any demonstration around him was contrived while yours was spontaneous? Probably. You and he saw the city so very differently! Was it as simple as 'law and order' versus 'peace?' You had spoken of your gathering the people as a hen protecting her brood; you would also lament the destruction coming upon them all.[45] O Jerusalem, that Foundation of Peace, how you have lost your way! You have not known *the time of your visitation from God!* Can we, with you and the prophet, claim peace that is coming? That *there is hope for the future, says the* Lord? How we, too, have missed *the things that make for peace.* Let us lament with you, our Lord, praying for peace on earth – proclaimed at your birth. Amen.

---

43   Luke 19:29-40
44   Herod kept seven palaces in Israel, moving constantly to avoid assassination.
45   Jerusalem would be besieged, overrun and leveled, 66-70 CE.

Friday, December 30, 2022

Fun Fact: In years Christmas falls on a Sunday, this 'Feast' moves to December 30

Read

Now every year his parents went to Jerusalem for the festival of the Passover. And when he was twelve years old, they went up as usual for the festival. When the festival was ended and they started to return, the boy Jesus stayed behind in Jerusalem, but his parents did not know it. Assuming that he was in the group of travelers, they went a day's journey. Then they started to look for him among their relatives and friends. When they did not find him, they returned to Jerusalem to search for him. After three days they found him in the temple, sitting among the teachers, listening to them and asking them questions. And all who heard him were amazed at his understanding and his answers. When his parents saw him they were astonished; and his mother said to him, "Child, why have you treated us like this? Look, your father and I have been searching for you in great anxiety." He said to them, "Why were you searching for me? Did you not know I must be in my Father's house?" But they did not understand what he said to them. Then he went down with them and came to Nazareth, and was obedient to them. His mother treasured all these things in her heart.
(Luke 2:41-52)

Reflect

We have in this account the first time Jesus is on record (in this synoptic Gospel) saying something his parents didn't understand. More was to come. The 'tween' Jesus (be-*tween* childhood and being a teenager) must have been so smart and yet so awkward as he worked to sort out being on this earth and heaven-sent for an eternal purpose. As he clearly understood and sought to understand the texts from the elders, he forgot that those around him didn't automatically know things. Jesus begins to set aside childish naïveté for informed servitude. How, in this new life as Christians, can we grow from learners to servants?

Pray

Our Lord and Savior, today we lift up this 'family story.' With your family, we marvel over who you have become – in a mere twelve years. Many families share stories of leaving a child behind – oh, the anguish! The frantic search! The overwhelming relief! And then... the accounting! They demanded to know: exactly what did you think you were doing? We know now that you were as 'centered' as any human being ever, even at twelve. You were nearing that 'age of accountability,' that cusp between childhood and adulthood. Families are never ready for that, are they? It is the moment when parents and children begin to see the world in profoundly different ways; 'tis ever thus. What was on the minds of Mary and Joseph as they hurried to Jerusalem? Remembering the good times? Or the 'unusual'? Dwelling on the worst? Blaming themselves? Finally, there you were! Amidst the elders there, we must not miss the shift from **this child** *listening to them and asking them questions* to **their** (the learned elders) being *amazed at his understanding and his answers.* The 'taught' became 'Teacher!' You had learned well in home and synagogue. In that moment, we lift up with thanksgiving dear Joseph and Mary, who *treasured all these things in her heart*, just as at your birth.[46] So may we, for you have come among us to dwell. Teach us, even us. Amen.

---

46   Luke 2:19

Saturday, December 31, 2022

Read

*Arise, shine; for your light as come,
and the glory of the Lord has risen upon you.*
(Isaiah 60:1)

Again Jesus spoke to them, saying, "I am the light of the world. Whoever follows me will never walk in darkness but will have the light of life." Then the Pharisees said to him, "You are testifying on your own behalf; your testimony is not valid." Jesus answered, "Even if I testify on my own behalf, my testimony is valid because I know where I have come from and where I am going, but you do not know where I come from or where I am going. You judge by human standards; I judge no one. Yet even if I do judge, my judgment is valid; for it is not I alone who judge, but I and the Father who sent me. In your law it is written that the testimony of two witnesses is valid. I testify on my own behalf, and the Father who sent me testifies on my behalf." Then they said to him, "Where is your Father?" Jesus answered, "You know neither me nor my Father. If you knew me, you would know my Father also."
(John 8:12-19)

Reflect

I like how Jesus says, "In your law…" Pharisees seem to struggle to get what we understand. There are your rules and then God's rules. Jesus tries to explain: God's rules are much simpler. In fact, they are as simple as light and dark. Want to know more? Follow me. Hang everything on my words because they come from not only me but from God.

Pray

O light of the world! In the northern hemisphere, as we claim the light in the midst of the darkest season, the contrast speaks to us. In the global south, the light is named on the longest days, days awash in light. You light it all, the dark and the day, even the dark places that threaten to overtake us: war, hunger, displacement, disease, violence. Here we remember your entanglement with some Pharisees who challenged your authority. Was it not just after you had saved the woman from a would be violent and surely fatal stoning?[47] Were any of these among her accusers? You name their penchant for judging by human standards, even as we note *no man* is indicted beside her. As you make a case for who you are, they do not find you to be a credible witness. Perhaps such a moment is prescient of proceedings to come. As they judge you, you state that you judge no one – but that you could, and validly, aligned as you are with the Father. For them then and for many now, your witness with the Father's is not enough. Would they then or others now accept the witness of the prophet?

Arise, shine; for your light as come,
and the glory of the L ORD *has risen upon you.*

We who claim to be your people, a people of the light, affirm you as you have said, *I am the light of the world.* Shine upon us, Lord Jesus! Amen.

---

47 John 8:1-11

First Sunday, January 1, 2023

Read

Now after they had left, an angel of the Lord appeared to Joseph in a dream and said, "Get up take the child and his mother, and flee to Egypt, and remain there until I tell you; for Herod is about to search for the child, to destroy him. Then Joseph got up, took the child and his mother by night, and went to Egypt, and remained there until the death of Herod. This was to fulfill what had been spoken by the Lord through the prophet, "Out of Egypt I have called my son." When Herod saw that he had been tricked by the wise men, he was infuriated, and he sent and killed all the children in and around Bethlehem who were two years old or under, according to the time that he had learned from the wise men. Then was fulfilled what had been spoken through the prophet Jeremiah:

*"A voice was heard in Ramah,
wailing and loud lamentation,
Rachel weeping for her children;
she refused to be consoled, because
they are no more."*

When Herod died, an angel of the Lord suddenly appeared in a dream to Joseph in Egypt and said, "Get up, take the child and his mother, and go to the land of Israel, for those who were seeking the child's life are dead." Then Joseph got up, took the child and his mother, and went to the land of Israel. But when he heard that Archelaus was ruling over Judea in place of his father Herod, he was afraid to go there. And after being warned in a dream, he went away to the district of Galilee. There he made his home in a town called Nazareth...
(Matthew 2:13-23a)

Reflect

We tell stories by relating them to other stories. Rachel, the mother of Benjamin, was buried not far from where Babylonian king Nebuchadnezzar gathered the people who made up a tribe (Benjamin) of this nation (Israel) and sent them into exile. Why such a horrible illustration of someone crying from beyond the grave for descendants who are "no more"? Because those who were in exile did return. Hope can arise from the tears and despair of a mother (Rachel) experiencing loss. Jesus the Messiah has been saved – and will save.

Pray

Lord, Savior – you were saved! We are in awe before the memory of Joseph and his dreams. From 'marrying Mary' to 'saving the Savior,' holy dreams guided him. Some will be distressed to consider our own dreams, where scattered pieces of life randomly scramble – incoherently. In that post-magi-moment, after the strange and wondrous eastern pilgrims had departed, Joseph awakened to the danger that was Herod. Surely others had spoken of the undercurrent in Herod's family, whose members dealt harshly, often fatally, with one another. Or had the magi mentioned their visit with Herod – and their expected return? Such things could have weighed upon Joseph as he lay down to sleep. When the angel said, 'flee!' he was ready to hear that and fled. How right he was! The horrific infanticide will live forever in notoriety. And you, Lord Jesus, would be an *émigré*, a *refugee*, and then a *returnee*. How we moderns skip over that! We view those who flee violence, who seek safety, who want only the well-being of their families as 'other,' or dangerous, even criminal. St Matthew's remembrance of Rachel's agony reminds us of the depth of human grief. Won't you help us see in the faces of those who seek safety your own face? You and your family have 'been there.' May we never forget! Amen.

Monday, January 2, 2023

Read

Now faith is the assurance of things hoped for, the conviction of things not seen…

By faith Abel offered to God a more acceptable sacrifice than Cain's. Through this he received approval as righteous, God himself giving approval of his gifts; he died, but through his faith he still speaks. By faith Enoch was taken so that he did not experience death; and 'he was not found because God had taken him.' For it was attested before he was taken away that 'he had pleased God.' And without faith it is impossible to please God, for whoever would approach him must believe that he exists and that he rewards those who seek him. By faith Noah, warned by God about events as yet unseen, respected the warning and built an ark to save his household; by this he condemned the world and became an heir to the righteousness that is in accordance with faith. By faith Abraham obeyed when he was called to set out for a place that he was to receive as an inheritance; and he set out, not knowing where he was going. By faith he stayed for a time in the land he had been promised, as in a foreign land, living in tents, as did Isaac and Jacob, who were heirs with him of the same promise. For he looked forward to a city that has foundations, whose architect and builder is God.
(Hebrews 11:1, 4-10)

Reflect

More stories from the scrolls to give us context. We hear of Cain and Able, Enoch, and Noah. All of this is wrapped up with a bow via the reminder of the faith of Abraham and Sarah. Jewish people of this time prided themselves in the faith of their ancestors, and rightfully so. All had very little 'visible' reason to believe in the promises or warnings from God but believed anyway. Specifically, Abraham's name comes up ten times in the book of Hebrews. Today we stand on the shoulders of these people of faith, as we have their examples of God's record of promises kept.

Pray

Lord Jesus, today we are in 'tall timber!' As children, we learn the stories of all these, coming to see them as heroes in the faith. We might wonder how it was that you learned of them. Were their stories read in the synagogue? Or told at home? In this season, as we continue to celebrate your coming, we might reflect on the ways in which you were 'formed,' your faith shaped and strengthened, even as your body grew. The writer in Hebrews offers us this:

Now faith is the assurance of things hoped for,
the conviction of things not seen.

Surely, our faith-forebears acted in such faith, that is, as travelers without a clear view of their destinations. We think of Abel with his offering; Enoch as he walked faithfully with God; Noah, afloat on the great unknown; Abram, journeying to a land he knew not, Isaac and Jacob after him. Neither did Mary and Joseph know the look of their destination. But faith, *the assurance of things hoped for, the conviction of things not seen* called them onward. May we in this moment let all that wash over us, refreshing in us such a faith; for our faith finally rests in you. Amen.

Tuesday, January 3, 2023

Read

Now faith is the assurance of things hoped for, the conviction of things not seen...
(Hebrews 11:1)

*Jacob left Beer-sheba and went towards Haran. He came to a certain place and stayed there for the night, because the sun had set. Taking one of the stones of the place, he put it under his head and lay down in that place. And he dreamed that there was a ladder set up on the earth, the top of it reaching to heaven; and the angels of God were ascending and descending on it. And the L*ord* stood beside him and said, 'I am the L*ord* the God of Abraham your father and the God of Isaac; the land on which you lie I will give to you and to your offspring; and your offspring shall be like the dust of the earth, and you shall spread abroad to the west and to the east and to the north and to the south; and all the families of the earth shall be blessed in you and in your offspring. Know that I am with you and will keep you wherever you go, and I will bring you back to this land; for I will not leave you until I have done what I promised you.' Then Jacob woke from his sleep and said, 'Surely the L*ord* is in this place – and I did not know it!' And he was afraid, and said, 'How awesome is this place! This is none other than the house of God, and this is the gate of heaven.'*
(Genesis 28:10-17)

Reflect

Some translations say ladder, others say stairway, and even others suggest that the original meaning is a ramp, but either way, a dream of angels of God ascending and descending doesn't mean much to us. Escalators, travelators (google it!), and elevators all represent the comings and goings of angels, but what do they convey? Does it have to do with future exiles? Or repatriation? How does that possibly help us today in our walk with the Lord? God's voice answers this. A promise made is a promise kept.

Pray

Lord, help us to hear the old story afresh. We pick it up where Jacob, son of Rebekah and Isaac, is on the run – for fear of his brother, an enraged Esau. As 'pottage'[48] grown too hot, the enmity between those twins had boiled over. Father Isaac sent Jacob, the blessed son (O Lord, why was there just one blessing?) for a wife from Uncle Laban's family; in so doing, he put some distance between him and his seething brother. Venturing into the great unknown, bone-weary, fearful and footsore, Jacob lay down to sleep. It is in that extremity, in that vulnerability in that strange place, that God comes to him in a dream. He 'sees' an earth-to-heaven ladder, a dream that Jacob will interpret, saying,

'How awesome is this place! This is none other than the house of God, and this is the gate of heaven.'

In this season, we note that this dreamer 'fathered' another dreamer, Joseph, whose gift of dreams would save the family *and* uncounted more. 'Our' gospel Joseph, his namesake, would also receive dreams from God: about your birth through Mary; fleeing to Egypt; returning to the homeland; moving once more for safety.[49] We are overwhelmed that Joseph saved you – that you might save us. The season has stirred in us our own 'dreams.' We pray that you help us use them to imagine anew what your lordship means for us and for a deeply troubled world. Save even us, Lord Jesus. Amen.

---

48 a sort of 'stew,' 'pottage' is from the KJV
49 Matthew 1:18-25; 2:13-23

Wednesday, January 4, 2023

Read

Now faith is the assurance of things hoped for, the conviction of things not seen...

By faith Moses was hidden by his parents for three months after his birth, because they saw that the child was beautiful; and they were not afraid of the king's edict. By faith Moses, when he was grown up, refused to be called the son of Pharaoh's daughter, choosing rather to share ill-treatment with the people of God than to enjoy the fleeting pleasures of sin. He considered abuse suffered for the Christ to be greater wealth than the treasures of Egypt, for he was looking ahead to the reward. By faith he left Egypt, unafraid of the king's anger; for he persevered as though he saw him who is invisible. By faith he kept the Passover and the sprinkling of blood, so that the destroyer of the firstborn would not touch the firstborn of Israel. By faith the people passed through the Red Sea as if it were dry land, but when the Egyptians attempted to do so they were drowned. By faith the walls of Jericho fell after they had been encircled for seven days. By faith Rahab the prostitute did not perish with those who were disobedient, because she had received the spies in peace.
(Hebrews 11:1, 23-31)

Reflect

The faith of our Heroes becomes our faith. The love of our God becomes our love. Can the peace of our Christ become our peace?

Pray

Our Lord and Savior, are there not many ways your own life calls to mind that of Moses? After all, Moses said, *The Lord your God will raise up for you a prophet like me from among your own people...*[50] The name 'Moses,' whose name suggests 'drawn from the water,' might also suggest your baptism; Moses, who stood against the empire of *his* day, just as you challenged Rome; treasures of Egypt or Rome, interested neither Moses nor you; once he claimed his identity, he, too, suffered abuse; he, too, was unafraid of the Pharaoh; he, too, kept the Passover – you became our Passover Lamb. Moses pointed to a God before whom the empire could not stand; ill-treatment of slaves could not stand; privileged position could not stand; the vast wealth of Egypt could not stand; the waters of the sea stood – they stood aside! The fortified walls of Jericho could not stand. But Moses stood, standing up, *for he persevered as though he saw him who is invisible.* Even one Rahab, standing apart from polite society, stood up! Did she not also 'persevere' *as though she saw him who is invisible*? As the prophets that followed in his faith steps, by faith, Moses spoke aloud the God-dream. So did you. So *do* you still. Amen.

---

50 Deuteronomy 18:15

Thursday, January 5, 2023

Read

Now faith is the assurance of things hoped for, the conviction of things not seen...

And what more should I say? For time would fail me to tell of Gideon, Barak, Samson, Jephthah, of David and Samuel and the prophets – who through faith conquered kingdoms, administered justice, obtained promises, shut the mouths of lions, quenched raging fire, escaped the edge of the sword, won strength out of weakness, became mighty in war, put foreign armies to flight. Women received their dead by resurrection. Others were tortured, refusing to accept release, in order to obtain a better resurrection. Others suffered mocking and flogging, and even chains and imprisonment. They were stoned to death, they were sawn in two, they were killed by the sword; they went about in skins of sheep and goats, destitute, persecuted, tormented – of whom the world was not worthy. They wandered in deserts and mountains, and in caves and holes in the ground. Yet all these, though they were commended for their faith, did not receive what was promised, since God had provided something better so that they would not, without us, be made perfect.

Therefore, since we are surrounded by so great a cloud of witnesses, let us also lay aside every weight and the sin that clings so closely, and let us run with perseverance the race that is set before us, looking to Jesus the pioneer and perfecter of our faith, who for the sake of the joy that was set before him endured the cross, disregarding its shame, and has taken his seat at the right hand of the throne of God.
(Hebrews 11:1, 32-12:2)

Reflect

A laundry list of the ways in which people of faith died wraps up our sojourn through Hebrews. A reminder that our heroes of the chosen people, and our heroes of Christ's story, have not always seen their deliverance at hand. We have the privilege of knowledge of what comes after the many sacrifices recounted. We know that God does not forget his faithful servants.

Pray

Our Lord, we find ourselves on the eve of the Epiphany, a time that will mark the season's change. The author of this epistle knew the stories, didn't he? For many of us, some of his accounting is too heavy to bear. These are they who seem to thrive in the zones of faith, defeating empires, making just the unjust, and Daniel-like, shutting the mouths of lions. We might admit that we know more about *weakness* than *strength out of weakness*. The recounting of those who suffered weighs heavily upon the faithful, even the ones who *escaped the edge of the sword.* How we would dearly love to *put foreign armies to flight* now. We know there are Christians persecuted even now, and they are not alone. Uighurs in China, Rohingya in Myanmar, and even our Jewish neighbors in the USA all suffer the slings and arrows of hatred for faith's sake. Where we are not faithful in prayer for any who are so persecuted, forgive us we pray. The epistle has named the nameless 'cloud of witnesses,' those who have run the race before us. Like them, we are charged to *lay aside every weight and the sin that clings so closely.*[51] We can scarcely imagine running our 'race' unencumbered, for the 'weights' are many. But with you, Lord Jesus, our Companion, our Encourager, our constant Friend, we run on! Amen.

---

51 Faith-ancestor John Wesley, 'Let us throw off whatever weighs us down, or damps the vigour of our soul." (Wesley's Notes on the New Testament)

Friday,
January 6, 2023, Epiphany

Read

*Arise, shine; for your light has come,
and the glory of the Lord has risen upon you.
(Isaiah 60:1)*

In the time of King Herod, after Jesus was born in Bethlehem of Judea, wise men from the East came to Jerusalem, asking, "Where is the child who has been born king of the Jews? For we observed his star at its rising, and have come to pay him homage." When King Herod heard this, he was frightened, and all Jerusalem with him; and calling together all the chief priests and scribes of the people, he inquired of them where the Messiah was to be born. They told him, "In Bethlehem of Judea; for so it has been written by the prophet: 'And you, Bethlehem, in the land of Judah, are by no means least among the rulers of Judah; for from you shall come a ruler who is to shepherd my people Israel.'" Then Herod secretly called for the wise men and learned from them the exact time when the star appeared. Then he sent them to Bethlehem, saying "Go and search diligently for the child; and when you have found him, bring me word so that I may also go and pay him homage." When they had heard the king, they set out; and there, ahead of them, went the star that they had seen at its rising, until it stopped over the place where the child was. When they saw that the star had stopped, they were overwhelmed with joy. On entering the house, they saw the child with Mary his mother; and they knelt down and paid him homage. Then opening their treasure chests, they offered him gifts of gold, frankincense, and myrrh. And having been warned in a dream not to return to Herod, they left for their own

country by another road.
(Matthew 2:1-12)

Reflect

As much as we can all complain about populist figures or brutal leaders in our days, there is no comparison to the hot, steaming pile of garbage that was King Herod. When Herod was sick and nearing death, he had many nobles arrested and planned for their execution to be the same day that he died. You see, Herod assumed that if many beloved people died on the same day as him, mourning would be more likely than massive parties. The inverse is a child, a baby, adored sight-unseen by people regarded as astrologers, foreign even to an Edomite like Herod. It is so telling that far-off Persians come to seek out a new king and merely -pit-stop' to see the earthly Herod. Let us join in the worshiping of the King of Kings, whom we recognize has joined us as the humble and powerless child.

Pray

Lord Jesus, we come to the end of our shared season of reflection and prayer together. Here we witness those filled with wisdom innocently collaborating with a king filled with evil – the heaven-sent and the hell-bent. We might say they were wise in many things, just not 'street-wise.' We note that the King called on still other wise ones, chief priests and scribes, to answer the question of the eastern visitors. This king would be completely unfamiliar with the idea of any *ruler who is to shepherd my people Israel.* We marvel at the time and, doubtless, the resources invested by these travelers. We might be struck that both the wise ones *and* the king are keenly interested in the newborn king, and both desire to *pay him homage.* Oh, how they mean vastly different things! On the one hand is honor, adoration, and gifts; on the other is certain dishonor and violent death. In an awful symmetry, you, Lord, will be threatened by 'a Herod' at birth *and* death. Did the wise men err by going to the king? What if they had questioned shepherds in fields nearby? Or an itinerant carpenter in the village? Or townspeople, perhaps an innkeeper, who might remember an odd circumstance not so long ago? We all tend to 'start at the top,' don't we? How will we ever learn that the 'God-dream' may not, *must* not align with the powerful, the privileged? With thankful hearts, we remember that the wise were dream-warned to leave by another way, and they did! With them and the prophet, we rejoice, saying,

Arise, shine; for your light has come,
and the glory of the L*ord* *has risen upon you.*

Want to Learn More?

Consider this publication by the same authors:
FastPrayGive: Ending Hunger By The Means Of Grace
  Pickup your copy at https://fastpraygive.org/store

www.ingramcontent.com/pod-product-compliance
Lightning Source LLC
Chambersburg PA
CBHW071910070526
44583CB00016B/1931